40DAY
SALES
DARE

FOR AUTO SALES

JASON FORREST

2013 Jason Forrest

For information or bulk orders, contact:
info@forrestpg.com

ForrestPG.com

Printed by MJS Press
Printed in the U.S.A.

International Standard Book Number: 978-0-9887523-6-8

DEDICATION —

*To the front-line sales pros who "bring it" every day—
the ones who make a choice in every moment and in
every interaction to be true X-Factor sales professionals.
You are the reason I do what I do.*

*And, as always, to my family. From Saunders and Mary
Jane (who teach me more than I teach them) to Shelly,
the love of my life. Thank you all.*

CONTENTS

Indicates that this Dare is a Day-Off Dare, meant to be executed when you are out of the office.

INTRODUCTION

Dear Sales Professional,

Are you ready to reach your full potential regardless of what market you're in and how many urgent buyers walk through your door each week? My vision for you is that each day of this 40-day journey brings you one step closer to the best version of you.

Whether you sought this book out or received it as a gift and/or assignment, it found you and will lead you to **earn what you're worth!**

Since your current performance is returning your current results, you can either keep doing everything the same way and wait for circumstances to tilt in your favor, or you can change your behaviors and therefore change your results.

This book will help you change your behaviors, but in order to get the most from the journey, I want you to focus on the following:

Take it one day at a time.

Rather than focusing on reaching the end of this book, the end of the quarter, or the end of the year, just commit to two things:
1. Reading each day's dare before you start your workday.
2. Executing each dare to the best of your ability. This is a mental and physical exercise—meaning you spend time to understand the section first and then execute the dare mentally and physically throughout the day.

See yourself as your only competitor.

Focus only on you and on your own game. Don't worry about your performance in comparison to anyone else's. Just work on being the best *you* you can be.

When you perceive that someone else is better than you, it's easy to lose hope in your potential and be defeated before you even begin. If you start to think that you will never become as good as someone else, you give yourself an unhealthy excuse not to challenge yourself.

It's just as dangerous to think you are better than someone else because you set a ceiling of what's possible for you and start thinking things like, "I'm selling 20% more than everyone else on my team—that must be good enough." The only thing that's truly "good enough" is your best. And you have the capacity to expand your best.

Your success is linear: As you improve your sales behaviors and beliefs, you improve your earnings, too.

Focus on each prospect as if he/she is your only customer.

Give each person who walks through the door the best version of you. Make a commitment to each of your future prospects (whose names and faces you have yet to learn) that you are going to give them the best experience you can. Live it out by slowing down and focusing on taking the person or people in front of you as far in the sales process as you can. Take it even further by considering each presentation once a client leaves. Consider what you did well and what you will do better with your next client.

Eliminate all excuses.

Whether you see thirty customers a day or zero, practice each dare each day. If you have thirty customers, perfect! Practice three times before anyone shows up, and then execute the dare with each one of those 30 prospects. You'll be a pro by the end of the 40-day journey. If you have zero customers, perfect! Practice the dare mentally, with your sales partner, and with your supervisor(s).

While we're at it, eliminate any excuse that pops into your head that tells you that you can't perform fully or don't have opportunity to practice each dare.

Make a commitment for the next forty days of your life not to worry about what can't be done, and not to say (or even think) that it's impossible to sell more in your situation.

One last thought.

In my first book, *Creating Urgency*, I discussed my belief that the desire to improve one's life has more influence over a person's buying decision than any other factor. I believe the same for you—the desire to improve your life has more influence over your decisions and behaviors than any other factor. So focus on how your life and your family's life will be better when you are better. Focus not on what you perceive as "impossible" in your circumstances, but rather on how to make things possible.

Give me forty days of your life, and let's see what happens together.

Your Sales Coach,

Jason

VERY IMPORTANT
DO NOT SKIP!

HOW TO USE THIS BOOK

SET UP

This book is designed to be used for forty successive days. That means that every day (whether you are going to work or not) you will have a dare to read and focus on.

Let's start with some vocabulary. For the purposes of this book, *Day-Off dares* are for those days when you are not scheduled to work. These can be done from anywhere. *Day-On dares* are for the days you do work.

LET'S GET TECHNICAL

The book is divided into six weeks (the last week is abbreviated). At the beginning of each week, you will see a page that lists the week's dares: *Five Day-On dares* and *two Day-Off dares*. This page is important because it helps you plan your week and determine which dare you should focus on each day. Here is an example of what that page will look like:

WEEK 1
Dares 1-7

Day-On Dares
_____ 1. A Spoonful of Sugar
_____ 2. All She Wanted was a
       Little Black Dress
_____ 3. Show Up
_____ 4. The Disneyland Treatment
_____ 5. Pick the Right Song

Day-Off Dares
_____ 6. Why Not?
_____ 7. It's Not a Used Tissue

VERY IMPORTANT
DO NOT SKIP!

To use this page, you will fill in your work schedule accordingly. I'm going to walk you through this, but first let me give you an example of how this works. Let's assume that you start *40 Day Sales Dare* on a Monday, and your days off are Tuesday and Wednesday.

Since your days off are Tuesday and Wednesday, you'll then jump to the Day-Off dares and write those days down. You'll then return to work on Thursday and pick back up with *dare 2*, continuing through to *dare 5* on Sunday. See below:

WEEK 1 EXAMPLE
Dares 1-7

Day-On Dares
Mon. 1. A Spoonful of Sugar
Thurs. 2. All She Wanted was a Little Black Dress
Fri. 3. Show Up
Sat. 4. The Disneyland Treatment
Sun. 5. Pick the Right Song

Day-Off Dares
Tues. 6. Why Not?
Wed. 7. It's Not a Used Tissue

YOU WRITE YOUR DAYS OFF
← HERE

Each week you have seven dares to complete—five for your days on and two for your days off. Each week you need to take a few seconds to plan your customized schedule for completing each of the week's seven dares. Now it's time for you to practice. I'll walk you through:

Week 1:

Step 1: Choose the day when you will begin *40 Day Sales Dare*. Be sure to choose a day when you will be in the office.

Step 2: Write that day next to the first Day-On dare of the week.

Step 3: Continue writing your "on" days next to the Day-On dares, until you come to your days off for the week.

Step 4: Write your "off" days next to the Day-Off dares.

Step 5: Finish filling in your "on" days for the week.

WEEK 1 FOR YOU
Dares 1-7

Day-On Dares

_____ 1. A Spoonful of Sugar

_____ 2. All She Wanted was a Little Black Dress

_____ 3. Show Up

_____ 4. The Disneyland Treatment

_____ 5. Pick the Right Song

Day-Off Dares

_____ 6. Why Not?

_____ 7. It's Not a Used Tissue

You've written your schedule for the first week! Unless your days off change, you'll probably stick to this same schedule each week. Now turn to page 17 to copy your schedule down and then ***return to page 14 for further instruction.***

NOTE: WEEK 6 WILL ONLY HAVE
FIVE DARES

What if I miss a day?

If you miss a day of work, you can adjust your *40 Day* schedule accordingly. Or, you can stay on the schedule you've created, and commit to making up the dare that you missed after you've completed dare 40. Whatever you decide to do, make sure that you only complete Day-On dares when you are at work.

TRACKING YOUR PROGRESS

When participating in any self-improvement program, it is vital to track your progress. Charting successes and shortcomings shows you where you are, where you need to go, and what you need to do in order to get there.

During your journey, you are going to track two important factors of your self-improvement: Effort and Potential Value.

Effort

Each dare concludes with an effort scale. You will be asked to rate the effort that you gave to executing the day's dare. Be honest—the purpose of this scale is to help you keep tabs on your commitment to the program. When you see yourself slipping, take corrective measures right away and recommit to earning what you're worth.

$ Potential Value $

At the end of each dare, you will also be asked what it was worth to you. That is, if you faithfully executed the dare each day, how many sales do you think it would earn you over the next year? You will circle a value on a scale that looks like this:

1   2   3   4   5   6   7   8

The purpose of this measurement is to help you focus on the future rewards that you will gain as a result of your efforts. Some dares will be challenging and will stretch you beyond your comfort zone, but if you can focus on the future increase in sales you will earn, you will be inspired to keep pressing forward in your journey toward self-improvement and success.

At the end of each week, you will see a **summary page** where you will be asked to calculate the average scores for your effort and your potential value. *It is critical that you complete this page.*

When you see your averages, you will know what kind of measures you need to take in order to conquer the next week. Doing this summary is like stepping on the scale every week to make sure that your diet and exercise routine is working—it's easier to make adjustments to lose one extra pound than it is to get back on the wagon four weeks later and attempt to lose the six pounds that mysteriously appeared.

TOTALING YOUR POTENTIAL

At the end of the book, you will calculate the total potential value of all forty dares. You will be able to say, "If I were to implement everything in this book, I would earn _____ sales in the coming year." Seeing this number in print will give you the motivation you need to take the dares to heart and to continue practicing them until you've mastered the concepts and strategies.

* * *

Now that you know how to use this book, it's time to get started. I hope you are ready for a life-changing journey.

Jason Forrest

WEEK ONE

Dares 1-7

DAY-ON DARES

_____1. A Spoonful of Sugar

_____2. All She Wanted Was a Little Black Dress

_____3. Show Up

_____4. The Disneyland Treatment

_____5. Pick the Right Song

DAY-OFF DARES

_____6. Why Not?

_____7. It's Not a Used Tissue

Give the customer a chance to become emotionally connected before you say that it's out of their price range.

DARE 1

A Spoonful of Sugar

READ

Picture this: a guy approaches a girl to ask her out. He says, "Hi, I'm Steve. I drink too much, smoke a pack a day, and eat more than I should. I don't work out, and I never remember birthdays or anniversaries. I won't be friends with your friends, but I expect you to be friends with mine. Oh, and one more thing—you must cook every meal." How likely is Steve to get a date? Even if Steve is speaking the truth, he'll have a lot better luck if he gets his potential date emotionally interested in him before he gives her a list of reasons to hate him.

It sounds extreme, but I see sales professionals do this all the time. They bring up stressful topics like credit scores, minimum down payments, and insurance prices before they even hand over a key for a test drive. Give your prospect a chance to fall in love with the heated seats and fuel efficiency before you say it's more money than they want to spend. Those discussions will come, but pace yourself. A little sugar goes a long way. Don't scare your customer off before the first date.

THINK

Think of a time in the past when you tried to dish out medicine before giving the customer enough sugar. How did that affect your sales experience with that customer?

_____

_____

_____

_____

DARE

I dare you today to make a list of all the questions or statements that could be perceived as negative or stressful to your customers. Make a point of discussing those topics only after your prospects have built an emotional connection to you and your product.

_____

_____

_____

_____

_____

_____

_____

_____

_____

REFLECT

1. Did you bring up anything negative or stressful prior to creating an emotional connection to you and your product? Circle one: YES   NO

   If yes, what did you say?

   _____

   _____

   _____

   _____

2. What effect did that have on your experience with the customer?

   _____

   _____

   _____

   _____

3. What can you do in the future to be more aware of the emotionally-negative questions and statements you are communicating to your customers before they have created a connection?

   _____

   _____

   _____

   _____

   _____

4. If you consistently executed this process with every prospect you see over the next year, how many sales would this dare earn you? Circle one:

1   2   3   4   5   6   7   8

EFFORT

Rate your effort level towards improving yourself today with this dare:

1   2   3   4   5   6   7   8   9   10

1: Did not read or do the dare. 2: Read the dare, but did not do it. 5: Did the dare with half of my customers today. 10: Did the dare with all customers today, and rehearsed the questions between customer encounters.

DARE 2

All She Wanted Was a Little Black Dress

READ

*M*y wife knew just what she wanted to wear to the formal New Year's Eve party. It was a special night, so she was looking for a special dress. In her mind, she saw something elegant—silky, strapless, and cut just above the knee. She went to four of her favorite department and specialty stores, but *her* dress just wasn't there.

Some were just a bit too short; others were the right length, but had straps. Some were the right shape and cut, but didn't come in black. She never did find what she had created in her mind, but did she buy something? Of course she did. It wasn't "perfect." It ended up being even better.

Your customer's vision is just the starting point, not the ending point. Don't kill yourself if you don't have exactly what they are looking for. Instead, focus on what you *do* have that is most similar to what they want. Your customers will end up buying the product that is closest to their needs, just like my wife's little black dress.

> MY CUSTOMER'S VISION IS JUST THE STARTING POINT, **NOT THE ENDING POINT**

THINK

Think back to your last major purchase. In what ways was it different from what you first pictured?

_____

_____

_____

Consider whether you were still happy with your decision. My guess is that you were, because otherwise, you wouldn't have signed on the dotted line. Your customers will be satisfied, too.

DARE

Today, focus less on finding the "perfect" product for your clients and more on finding the best product for their needs.

_____

_____

_____

_____

_____

_____

_____

_____

_____

_____

REFLECT

1. In what ways did it remove pressure from you when you stopped focusing on having the "perfect" product for your customers?

_____

_____

_____

_____

_____

2. In what ways were you able to demonstrate your product to more of your customers by not having to eliminate ones that weren't "perfect" for what they described? Note: If you did not have any customers, then consider when you have eliminated customers in the past.

_____

_____

_____

_____

_____

3. Do you have any success stories of a customer who ended up liking something different from what they initially said they wanted? Note: If you don't have an example from today, then write down an example of a past customer.

_____

_____

_____

_____

4. Considering that there is no such thing as a "perfect" product, why are customers' initial "wants" a moving target?

_____

_____

_____

_____

_____

5. If you consistently executed this process with every prospect you see over the next year, how many sales would this dare earn you? Circle one:

1   2   3   4   5   6   7   8

EFFORT

Rate your effort level towards improving yourself today with this dare:

1   2   3   4   5   6   7   8   9   10

_____

1: Did not read or do the dare. 2: Read the dare, but did not do it. 5: Did the dare with half of my customers today. 10: Did the dare with all customers today, and rehearsed the questions between customer encounters.

DARE 3

Show Up

READ

Woody Allen, American film director, says, "Eighty percent of success is showing up." In sales, showing up physically *and* mentally automatically increases your chances for success.

"Showing up" in new car sales means consistently doing those daily tasks that often fall by the wayside: wiping fingerprints off windows, vacuuming after test drives, and most of all—making those follow-up calls every day. We'll focus on that last one today.

If you've been in the business long enough, you already know that the sheer act of picking up the phone increases your sales. Even though it's tempting to feel like you've done all you can after you give your prospect the best possible presentation, follow-up calls are crucial to your success. The truth is that 85% of customers leave the house intent on buying a vehicle, so every minute that passes from the time they leave your office gets *somebody* closer to the sale.

38% of customers purchase within 4 hours of visiting their first dealership.

57% of consumers purchase within 3 days of visiting their first dealership.

90% of customers purchase within 1 week of visiting their first dealership.*

If you have a competitive streak (and you're in sales, so you probably do), then think of it as a race between you and your competition—first one to lead the customer to a solution within the first week wins!

By picking up the phone, you've already shown up physically, but there's a bit more to the story. Now it's time to show up mentally. The prevalence of texting, Instagram, and other forms of immediate communication makes for a society of chronic multi-taskers. You can tell when your spouse or friend is multi-tasking and disengaged from the conversation, right? Hint: your customers can, too. Distractions are inevitable, but you can do your part by turning off your cell phone, closing your e-mail, and telling your coworkers that you are making follow-up calls and are not to be disturbed.

When you call your prospects, picture yourself sitting next to them. You wouldn't check your e-mail, surf the web, or play computer solitaire if they were sitting beside you. Refraining from these activities while you're on the phone allows you to focus intently on what your prospects say and on how they say it. The customer *must* feel that you are tuning the world out and tuning them in!

Listen to Woody Allen (he's a very successful fellow, after all) and show the heck up today.

THINK

Schedule a 60-minute time slot for your follow-up calls, and set it as a recurring appointment in your calendar each week.

PICTURE MYSELF SITTING NEXT TO MY CLIENT

*NADA Studies

DARE

I dare you to spend one hour calling prospects today. Place enough prospect cards in front of you to take you through the whole hour. Tip: You should have at least 25 prospects available as you will have some unanswered calls. If you go through all of your predetermined calls before the time is up, pull out a new stack. Keep going until the whole hour is done.

REFLECT

1. How many calls did you make today? _____

2. How many people did you speak to today? _____

3. How many appointments did you make today? _____

4. What percentage of the 60 minutes did you use to make your phone calls today?

_____%

Note: If the answer is 100%, then congratulate yourself for investing in your career and move on to question 5.

For anything less than 100%, consider why you didn't make the calls:
    a. It was uncomfortable.
    b. I was afraid of the answer.
    c. I forgot.
    d. I didn't want to.

5. What did you learn about your customers by calling them? Write out a specific example.

_____

_____

_____

_____

_____

_____

_____

_____

6. By making the calls, were you better equipped to accomplish your customers' goals and, in so doing, to improve their lives? How?

_____

_____

_____

_____

_____

7. If you consistently executed this process with every prospect you see over the next year, how many sales would this dare earn you? Circle one:

1   2   3   4   5   6   7   8

EFFORT

Rate your effort level towards improving yourself today with this dare:

1   2   3   4   5   6   7   8   9   10

_____

1: Did not read or do the dare. 2: Read the dare, but did not do it. 5: Did the dare with half of my customers today. 10: Did the dare with all customers today, and rehearsed the questions between customer encounters.

DARE 4

The Disneyland Treatment

READ

*I*magine yourself and a wee companion (maybe your child, niece, or nephew) on a Disneyland tour. You're in search of hidden treasure, but along the way, there are rides to ride, magical worlds to explore, and characters to meet. Your tour guide takes her time, pointing out each exciting feature along the way and snapping photographs of the kids shaking hands with Mickey Mouse. However, she steers clear of a popular roller-coaster that is under repair at the moment. She takes great care in creating the best experience possible because she wants your young companion to remember meeting Mickey, not the disappointment of having to skip Gadget's Go Coaster.

Think of yourself as a Disneyland tour guide (minus the Mickey Mouse hat), and remember that the path is as important as the destination. The path can be everything from the route that allows you to stroll past the recently-polished vehicles rather than the dusty trade-ins you just got in to the exact

THE JOURNEY IS THE
DESTINATION

moment you unveil the hands-free mobile feature. Think about it even for your test drive. Direct your prospects on a route that is visually appealing and that also allows them to test the car's brakes and power. Consider your customer's experience in every aspect of your presentation.

You and the Disneyland tour guide share a common mission: to create the best perception possible of your little corner of the world.

THINK

Take a look around your dealership today, making note (with pen and paper or digitally, not just mentally) of everything that portrays a positive feeling about your dealership. Look through the eyes of a customer. Consider the areas you'd like to spiff up and/or avoid as well. Drive the surrounding streets and pretend like you're seeing them for the first time. The Disneyland treatment takes customers along the prettiest route and allows them to test their future car's awesome features.

DARE

I dare you today to take every customer along your planned route and re-plan your course as things change.

REFLECT

1. Why do you believe you or other sales professionals in the past have not given each customer the "Disneyland" treatment?

_____

_____

_____

_____

_____

DARE 4: THE DISNEYLAND TREATMENT

2. What did you do differently with your prospects today because of this dare?

_____

_____

_____

_____

_____

3. How did it improve their experience?

_____

_____

_____

_____

_____

4. By looking at your dealership and the surrounding area in this way, what did you learn that you would not have known otherwise?

_____

_____

_____

_____

_____

5. If you consistently executed this process with every prospect you see over the next year, how many sales would this dare earn you? Circle one:

1   2   3   4   5   6   7   8

EFFORT

Rate your effort level towards improving yourself today with this dare:

1 2 3 4 5 6 7 8 9 10

———————————————

1: Did not read or do the dare. 2: Read the dare, but did not do it. 5: Did the dare with half of my customers today. 10: Did the dare with all customers today, and rehearsed the questions between customer encounters.

DARE 5

Pick the Right Song

READ

Year after year, a few contestants on reality shows like *American Idol* and *The Voice* hear one phrase from the judges: "Pick the right song." *Not* picking the right song has been the kiss of death for many talented, hardworking, and highly motivated contestants.

Remember Brooke White? Even vaguely? Though her voice was stellar, her name was lost in the unmemorable ghosts of contestants past. How about Lil Rounds? Week after week, the judges dinged the 2009 contestant for choosing songs that weren't right for her unique style and voice. Contestants do best when they select songs that allow them to perform in their element.

Contestants with superstar potential end up watching the rest of the season from their couches. So what separates these hardworking vocalists from the ones in the finale? Picking the right song.

The same thing happens to sales professionals. Sometimes talented, hardworking, and highly motivated people end up lost in the mix of a customer's search because the sales pro picks the wrong song. What does the wrong song mean for you as a sales pro?

It means you present a solution to a prospect's problem b*efore* you really understand what the customer is looking for. As a result, your "performance" misses the mark and falls flat. As a sales pro, you really have to understand each person's unique needs before you start presenting the solution.

You can gain that understanding by finding out what's wrong with your customers' current situation, why they need a new car in the first place, and what will most improve their lives.

In so doing, you stand out as a contestant who chose the right song, and it will make you more likely to get your customers' votes.

THINK

Think back to the last time you started selling before you really understood what the customer needed. Mentally retrace your steps through the interaction, from the moment you saw them pull up to the time they left. Is the picture coming back to you? Okay, what was one feature or benefit you sold before you truly knew what the client wanted? Now visualize the same car pulling up again, and walk through what you would do differently today. Describe the alternative scenario below.

_____

_____

_____

_____

_____

_____

_____

_____

DARE 5: PICK THE RIGHT SONG

_____
_____
_____
_____
_____
_____
_____
_____
_____
_____
_____

DARE

I dare you today to *really* understand what each customer needs prior to showing your products. You can accomplish this by asking the following questions to every prospect:

1. What is it about your current car that you want to change?
2. What's gotten you thinking about looking for something new?

Before the day starts, and between each customer visit, say the questions aloud so that you memorize them and feel comfortable using them. Remember, the goal is to start showing or describing your product only after you know that you have something that will improve your prospects' lives.

I NEED TO UNDERSTAND MY CUSTOMER'S UNIQUE NEEDS BEFORE I CAN PRESENT THE SOLUTION

REFLECT

1. How did asking these two questions change your performance today?

_____

_____

_____

_____

_____

_____

_____

2. How did it feel to dig deeper with these questions?

_____

_____

_____

_____

_____

_____

_____

_____

3. With what percentage of your customers did you use both questions?

_____%

Note: If the answer is 100%, then congratulate yourself for investing in your career, and move on to question 4.

For anything less than 100%, consider why you didn't ask the questions to each customer:

    a. It was uncomfortable.
    b. I was afraid of the answer.
    c. I forgot.
    d. I didn't want to.

4. What did you learn about your customers from using these questions?

_____

_____

_____

_____

_____

5. Most importantly, did you hold off describing and showing your product until you *knew* that you had something that would improve the customer's life? Circle one: YES   NO

If yes, how did that help you? If no, what will you do differently next time?

_____

_____

_____

_____

6. If you consistently executed this process with every prospect you see over the next year, how many sales would this dare earn you? Circle one:

1   2   3   4   5   6   7   8

EFFORT

Rate your effort level towards improving yourself today with this dare:

1   2   3   4   5   6   7   8   9   10

1: Did not read or do the dare. 2: Read the dare, but did not do it. 5: Did the dare with half of my customers today. 10: Did the dare with all customers today, and rehearsed the questions between customer encounters.

WEEK 1

DAY-OFF DARES

If you don't believe you can be better, then there is no motivation for you to labor for your goals. Believe in yourself.

DAY OFF

DARE 6

Why Not?

READ

Mia Michaels, Emmy Award-winning choreographer best known for her work on Fox TV's *So You Think You Can Dance*, has seen her pieces performed by Cirque du Soleil, Madonna, and Celine Dion, among others. When asked if it was intimidating to keep creating better dance routines, she said, "Absolutely! But as soon as it stops getting challenging to recreate and I get bored, then it's time to retire." Just think about that. It's a mindset that welcomes challenge and thrives on rising above circumstances. It's a mindset that works.

The top politicians, leaders, businesspeople, dancers, and musicians are not likely to get to the top by asking, "Why me?" or "How could I possibly be the one to reach such a pinnacle?" If they don't believe they can be better, then there is no motivation to prepare and to labor for their goals. It's likely they won't go through the pain if they don't believe they can have the gain.

**HOW CAN I
OVERCOME THIS?**

THINK

How much do your beliefs affect what you do and think? Do you believe it's possible to do anything that is incongruent with your beliefs?

What would happen to your actions and behaviors if you started saying, "Why not?" rather than, "Of course not"? How would you approach your day differently if you responded to challenges not by asking, "Why?" but by asking, "How can I overcome this?"

_____

_____

_____

_____

_____

_____

_____

_____

_____

_____

_____

_____

_____

_____

_____

DARE

Today I dare you to make two lists. Under "The average salesperson believes..." write down all of the phrases you have said or heard people say in the past that caused you to doubt yourself and/or your ability to sell. Under "I believe..." write the beliefs you would like to adopt—the beliefs that make you better. Make three copies of these lists, and put a set in your bathroom, in your office, and on your refrigerator.

Starting today, read the "I believe" list out loud. Every time you or someone else says something from the average salesperson's list, then consciously replace that phrase with one from your "I believe" list.

REFLECT

1. How would your sales results (or life) be different if you were living by your "I believe" statements all the time?

_____

_____

_____

_____

_____

_____

2. If you consistently executed this belief process every day over the next year, how many sales would this dare earn you? Circle one:

1   2   3   4   5   6   7   8

THE AVERAGE SALESPERSON BELIEVES	I BELIEVE

DARE 6: WHY NOT?

EFFORT

Rate your effort level towards improving yourself today with this dare:

1   2   3   4   5   6   7   8   9   10

_____

1: Did not read or do the dare. 2: Read the dare, but did not do it. 5. Did the dare with minimal effort. 10: Did the dare with 100% effort.

DAY OFF

DARE 7

It's Not a Used Tissue

READ

*I*n *Creating Urgency,* I focused on one main premise: **The desire to improve one's life has more influence over a person's buying decision than any other factor.** When this idea first struck me, I revered the thought and unveiled the line like a fine work of art. Since then, I've explained the concept before large audiences and on thousands of coaching calls. On a recent sales visit of my own, I threw the line out there as an afterthought. When my audience started scrambling to write it down, I realized that I treated the line I once saw as a jewel more like a used tissue. The revelation was just as powerful as it had been to me when it first hit me. The line wasn't stale, but my delivery was.

This is a common pitfall in all performance-based careers. We confuse our perception with the customer's perception, and we neglect the very features that give us our edge. Your customers have never experienced what you see every day, so think about those unique qualities, special touches, and hidden gems that set your product, dealership, and manufacturer apart. Remember these jewels and deliver the lines with the same reverence you did when you first discovered their value.

IS MY DELIVERY STALE?

THINK

Do you revere the special features and qualities of your product and manufacturer today just as much as you did the first time you discovered them? If so, do your actions reflect that reverence? Why or why not?

_____

_____

_____

_____

_____

_____

_____

_____

_____

_____

_____

_____

DARE

I dare you to treat every customer this week as if it were the first time they'd ever seen you, your product, and your manufacturer and to speak as if it were the first time you'd ever gotten the chance to share everything that makes your product great.

REFLECT

1. Write out some specific features of your product and manufacturer that you feel you need to present as "brand new" to your prospects. What makes these features so special? When you really believe in their value, you'll sell it that way.

_____

_____

_____

_____

_____

_____

_____

_____

_____

2. How did renewing your perception about your special features affect the way you think about your sales process?

_____

_____

_____

_____

_____

_____

3. If you consistently took ownership over creating urgency with every prospect you see in the next year, how many sales would this dare earn you? Circle one:

1   2   3   4   5   6   7   8

EFFORT

Rate your effort level towards improving yourself today with this dare:

1   2   3   4   5   6   7   8   9   10

1: Did not read or do the dare. 2: Read the dare, but did not do it. 5. Did the dare with minimal effort. 10: Did the dare with 100% effort.

PAUSE HERE!

WEEK 1 SUMMARY

*B*efore you continue in your journey towards improvement, take a moment to get your bearings by completing your Week 1 Summary. **You must do this before you continue to Week 2.**

Average Effort Score for Week 1:

Review your Effort Scores from dares 1-7, and calculate your Average Effort Score for the week. Write it in the space below.

---

4 or less = It's time to get serious. Recommit yourself to the program, and start fresh in Week 2 by striving for a 5 or higher each day!

5 to 7 = You're off to a strong start, but you can do even better! Make a commitment today to raise the bar for yourself in Week 2, and strive for an average of 8 or better.

8 to 9 = What a great start! Keep pushing forward, and make it your personal goal to score all 9's and 10's in Week 2.

10 = Excellent! You are a rock star. If you maintain this effort level, you will receive the maximum benefit from this program and you will achieve the success you desire.

What's it worth?

What was this week worth to you? Flip back through Week 1, and tally the number of sales that you said dares 1-7 would earn you. Write it below.

_____

7 dares down...33 to go!
You can do it!

WEEK TWO

Dares 8–14

DAY-ON DARES

____8. Let's Go for a Ride

____9. Tell Me About Your Current Situation

____10. K.I.S.S.: Keep It Short and Simple

____11. Emotions Stick

____12. You Can Handle the Truth

DAY-OFF DARES

____13. You or Circumstance?

____14. More Than Words

Remember: the desire to improve one's life has more influence over a customer's buying decision than any other factor.

DARE 8

Let's Go for a Ride

READ

What if you could go for a ride in each of your customers' current cars and watch their routine day after day? You could just sit in the back and observe while a couple struggles to find the right temperature or while a dad tries to juggle groceries while digging for his keys. You could catch them sharing about the features they love and overhear their casual comments like, "Our next car just *has* to have x, y, and z."

If you could observe prospects on a daily basis, you'd be completely prepared to address their needs, wouldn't you? I'm not trying to get you arrested for stalking here. So for our purposes, you'll have to settle for the next best thing: Having your customers mentally walk you through their challenges. Ask questions like the following:

1. Why did you choose your current car?
2. What is your favorite feature of your car?
3. If you could change just one thing about your car, what would it be?

As you ask these questions (and don't pigeonhole yourself here; there are plenty more questions that give insight), your customer will have the opportunity to lay out all of the problems with their current situation. That makes your job easy: offer solutions. If they told you that they just can't live without dual climate control, you can deliver that wish. People aren't going to argue with their own advice.

OFFER SOLUTIONS

THINK

In what ways would it be easier to find the right product for prospects if you were able to observe their daily lives?

DARE

I dare you today to ask each of the questions above to every customer you see today. When you don't have customers in front of you, practice saying the questions aloud.

Tip: To prepare yourself for a stronger follow-up, be sure to write your prospects' answers on their registration card or prospect sheet.

REFLECT

1. Did you ask each of your prospects the three questions today? If yes, how did it go? If no, why not?

_____

_____

_____

_____

_____

2. How did asking these questions help you tailor your sales presentation to your customers?

_____

_____

_____

_____

_____

_____

_____

3. What will you do in the future to remind yourself to ask more questions about your customers' current situation?

_____

_____

_____

_____

_____

_____

_____

4. If you consistently executed this process with every prospect you see over the next year, how many sales would this dare earn you? Circle one:

1   2   3   4   5   6   7   8

EFFORT

Rate your effort level towards improving yourself today with this dare:

1   2   3   4   5   6   7   8   9   10

1: Did not read or do the dare. 2: Read the dare, but did not do it. 5: Did the dare with half of my customers today. 10: Did the dare with all customers today, and rehearsed the questions between customer encounters.

"You are the catalyst for a customer's decision-making process."
—Creating Urgency

DARE 9

Tell Me About
Your Current Situation

READ

Yesterday (or on your last day on), we talked about getting your customer to take you with them on their daily drives. Now that you're nice and comfortable asking questions about their challenges, we'll focus on something that is just as important for some. It's the same concept, but this time you want them to walk you mentally through their situation. The goal is to understand fully what they like and dislike about it. You'll ask questions regarding what features they have (and which they want), what they like about their current car (and what they'd like to change), and what they feel their manufacturer is great at (and what they lack).

Whatever you're asking, the goal is to position yourself to understand what your customer needs. This gives you a head start in the race to accomplish your customer's mission. Oh yes, this is a race. The sales professional who most quickly and completely understands the customer's mission, and then solves it the fastest, is the sales pro who wins the deal.

THINK

How will the customers' likes and dislikes concerning their current situation influence their next purchase?

_____

_____

_____

_____

_____

_____

_____

_____

DARE

I dare you today to ask at least three of the following questions to every customer you see. When you don't have customers in front of you, practice saying the questions aloud.

- How long have you had your current car?
- How many vehicles and manufacturers did you consider before you chose your current car?
- Besides the car itself, what other factors influenced your decision?
- What is your spouse's favorite feature of your car?
- What is your child's/children's favorite feature of your car?
- What features in your car are you not using?
- What features do you wish your current car had?

THIS IS A
RACE

REFLECT

1. What did you learn about your customers' future needs by asking questions about their current likes and dislikes? Note: Be sure to jot their answers on their information card to reference in your follow-up calls.

_____

_____

_____

_____

_____

_____

_____

2. How did asking those questions influence your sales presentation?

_____

_____

_____

_____

_____

_____

3. If you consistently executed this process with every prospect you see over the next year, how many sales would this dare earn you? Circle one:

1   2   3   4   5   6   7   8

EFFORT

Rate your effort level towards improving yourself today with this dare:

1   2   3   4   5   6   7   8   9   10

———————————

1: Did not read or do the dare. 2: Read the dare, but did not do it. 5: Did the dare with half of my customers today. 10: Did the dare with all customers today, and rehearsed the questions between customer encounters.

DARE 10

K.I.S.S.:
Keep It Short and Simple

READ

"*I* have only made this letter rather long because I have not had time to make it shorter."—Blaise Pascal, 1662

Pascal, the French mathematician and philosopher, understood a concept many writers including Henry David Thoreau, T.S. Eliot, and Mark Twain have since echoed: The fewer the words, the better. Simplicity works both in writing and in follow-up calls because the more you talk, the less people remember.

After you've engaged your prospect on the phone, cut right to the chase and use the following three-step script:

- Summarize what you and the customer have accomplished so far.
- Tell them what comes next.
- Set up an appointment to make the next step.

After you've summarized the accomplishments, the next step goes something like this:

"The next thing we need to do is go back to the two products you liked and decide which one is a better fit for your family." *Or* "The next thing I would like to do is cover our great financing options and show you how easy it is to buy a car."

Say what you need to say, schedule the next action, and then get off the phone. Do what my editor tells me to do when she thinks I'm being long-winded: Keep it short and simple (K.I.S.S.).

THINK

Why do you and/or other sales professionals cover too much detail over the phone instead of just cutting to the chase? How would it benefit you if you were in the customer's shoes and a sales pro used the three-step script?

DARE

I dare you to call at least five prospects today. To prepare, write out your simple three-step script for each prospect prior to calling them. (Summarize what you and the customer have accomplished so far, tell them what comes next, and then set up an appointment to make it happen.)

REFLECT

1. How many of the five calls did you make today? _____ calls.
   Note: If the answer is all five, then congratulate yourself for investing in your career and move on to question 2. If you made fewer than five calls, consider why you didn't make them:

   a. I was unprepared.
   b. I was afraid that I was going to bother the prospect.
   c. I forgot.
   d. I didn't want to.

2. How did using the three-step script feel? Did it make your follow-up calls more productive?

_____

_____

_____

_____

_____

_____

_____

_____

3. What did you learn about your customers by calling them?

_____

_____

_____

_____

4. By making the calls and following the three-step script, were you better equipped to accomplish your customers' goals and, in so doing, to improve their lives?

_____

_____

_____

5. If you consistently executed this process with every prospect you see over the next year, how many sales would this dare earn you? Circle one:

1   2   3   4   5   6   7   8

EFFORT

Rate your effort level towards improving yourself today with this dare:

1   2   3   4   5   6   7   8   9   10

———————————

1: Did not read or do the dare. 2: Read the dare, but did not do it. 5: Did the dare with half of my customers today. 10: Did the dare with all customers today, and rehearsed the questions between customer encounters.

DARE 11

Emotions Stick

READ

*I*t was my first time meeting the "real" Mickey Mouse. I ate cotton candy, and my dad carried me around the park on his shoulders. I can almost hear "It's a Small World After All" as I write. It was my first visit to Disney World and the Epcot Center. I was eight.

How can I picture this image so vividly 23 years later, when I can't even remember where I park the car at the movie theater? Because emotions stick.

Big-ticket purchases are emotional, so get your prospects to visualize how they are going to use the car—where the kids will sit and how they'll use each feature. Tell them, "This will help me understand how you will use the vehicle, which will help me find the best one for you. Let's go through the features together and talk about how and when you will use them." As you open the door, say, "I need you to tell me how the car feels. You and I both know that if it doesn't feel right, it's probably not the one for you."

Then open the door, wait five seconds, and ask how the vehicle feels. If the reaction is positive, continue the sales process. If the customer's first impressions are iffy, then ask why it doesn't feel quite right.

As you test drive the car say, "Okay, I want this to be interactive, so let's talk about x, y, z features."

Succeed at getting your prospects emotionally involved, and you're halfway there.

THINK

Your clients aren't just buying a car. They're buying something that will make them feel safe at 75 miles an hour and will get their kids safely from school to basketball practice. They're not buying a product. They're buying a life improvement. Sell it that way.

DARE

I dare you today to focus on getting each customer emotionally involved with the product that best suits their needs. Use the above script, and use it with each customer you speak to today. In between customer visits, rehearse the script and visualize sending your customers home with their new car.

BIG-TICKET PURCHASES ARE
EMOTIONAL

REFLECT

1. How did using the script feel? What can you do to feel more comfortable using it?

_____

_____

_____

_____

DARE 11: EMOTIONS STICK

_____

_____

_____

_____

_____

_____

_____

2. With what percentage of your customers did you use the script?

_____%

Note: If the answer is 100%, then congratulate yourself for investing in your career, and move on to question 3. For anything less than 100%, consider why you didn't ask each question to each customer:

    a. It was uncomfortable.
    b. I was afraid of the answer.
    c. I forgot.
    d. I didn't want to.

3. How did this dare work for you today?

_____

_____

_____

_____

_____

4. By focusing on the emotional side of the decision, how were you able to create closer connections with each prospect?

_____

_____

_____

_____

_____

_____

_____

5. If you consistently executed this process with every prospect you see over the next year, how many sales would this dare earn you? Circle one:

1   2   3   4   5   6   7   8

EFFORT

Rate your effort level towards improving yourself today with this dare:

1   2   3   4   5   6   7   8   9   10

_____

1: Did not read or do the dare. 2: Read the dare, but did not do it. 5: Did the dare with half of my customers today. 10: Did the dare with all customers today, and rehearsed the questions between customer encounters.

The objections your prospects cite and their true concerns are not always the same thing.

DARE 12

You Can Handle the Truth

READ

*O*bjections are as much a part of your job as they are for any judge in a courtroom. For you, they're the reasons your customers don't want to move forward with their purchase. The trouble is that the objections your prospects cite and their true concerns are not always the same thing. Your challenge, then, is to seek out the true reason for each objection you hear today.

As a professional, it's your job to understand the real objection behind the spoken objection—don't just respond to the stated concern. This assures that you maintain credibility with the prospects and earn their trust to continue with them on their car-buying journey.

Picture the following scenario: You're talking to a customer. They're engaged in the discussion, you're in the rhythm, and you're feeling fine. Then, for some reason, they tell you that they're not so sure they want your product after all. *They liked it five minutes ago*, you think, so you launch into all the reasons why your product is so perfect. You make a foolproof case, but then they utter the dreaded six words, "We need to think about it."

Why? Because you handled the wrong objection. You thought they did not like the overall manufacturer; that is, after all, what they seemed to be saying. However, that was not their true concern. If you'd have taken the time to dig a little deeper, you would have discovered that they do like your manufacturer; but they're concerned that the car you showed them may not have great resale value. You did not seek the true concern, so you missed your opportunity to address it.

Today, whenever your prospects hesitate about your manufacturer, cars, or features, dig a little deeper and ask clarifying questions that help you uncover the real objection before you start defending your position.

The good news is that your prospects aren't on the stand in a courtroom, and they *want* you to know what they're looking for. So do them a favor, and ask them questions that help them communicate what they already want you to know.

That's right. You *can* handle the truth. And you must.

THINK

When was the last time you answered the spoken objection before seeking the true objection? Were you afraid of the customer's concern? Did you think you understood the objection, only to find out later that you didn't?

_____

_____

_____

_____

_____

_____

_____

_____

_____

_____

_____

_____

_____

Conversely, think of an example of a time when you asked clarifying questions and discovered that the objections weren't as hard to address as you thought they were. If you've been selling on your own for a week, or a decade, you've probably missed out on similar situations by not seeking the truth.

_____

_____

_____

_____

_____

_____

_____

_____

_____

_____

DIG DEEPER & UNCOVER THEIR TRUE CONCERN

DARE

I dare you today to seek the truth behind the objection. Use clarifying questions such as, "Why are you concerned about x, y, and z?" and "What is it about the manufacturer (color, size, etc.) that bothers you?"

Don't just start talking without understanding the true objection. The best way to ensure that you have successfully sought the truth is to restate what you heard back to the customer. Whether you are right or wrong, the customer will tell you.

REFLECT

1. Did you seek the truth behind every objection? Explain.

_____

_____

_____

_____

_____

_____

2. Did you ask clarifying questions to understand the true objection?
Circle one: YES   NO

If no, then why? If yes, then write down the questions you used.

_____

_____

_____

_____

_____

3. Were you able to resolve the objection? Circle one: YES   NO

If yes, how was the process different from what you've done in the past? If not, then why?

_____

_____

_____

_____

_____

_____

4. If you consistently executed this process with every prospect you see over the next year, how many sales would this dare earn you? Circle one:

1   2   3   4   5   6   7   8

EFFORT

Rate your effort level towards improving yourself today with this dare:

1   2   3   4   5   6   7   8   9   10

1: Did not read or do the dare. 2: Read the dare, but did not do it. 5: Did the dare with half of my customers today. 10: Did the dare with all customers today, and rehearsed the questions between customer encounters.

WEEK 2

DAY-OFF DARES

**"We cannot allow ourselves to be
victims of circumstance."**
—*Creating Urgency*

DAY OFF

DARE 13

You or Circumstance?

READ

I n my years of training and coaching, I have never seen a sales professional performing perfectly and not selling. That's why I don't buy it when I hear sales professionals say, "The market is tough. I just don't know what else to do," followed closely by, "I'm just too busy to do the sales training that you want me to do."

It doesn't make sense to complain about the outside circumstances affecting your success, and then say there isn't enough time to improve your skills. The next time you start to complain about the market or your inventory, think instead about your performance and what *you* can *do* to overcome those circumstances. What training can you take? What book can you read? What person can you learn from? Once you invest 100% in your improvement, see what happens to your sales.

THINK

Why do you believe you (or other sales professionals) have said there isn't enough time to go through training , while also complaining about not getting enough sales?

DARE

I dare you today to reflect on what you have said and thought since you first opened this book. Have you said that you don't have time to do the dares, and at the same time complained that you are not selling as much as you need to? I dare you to put 100% effort into every dare from this day forward.

WHAT CAN I DO TO OVERCOME MY CIRCUMSTANCES?

REFLECT

1. What can you do to hold yourself accountable to focusing first on a perfect sales presentation before complaining that it is impossible to sell more in your circumstances?

_____

_____

_____

_____

_____

_____

_____

_____

_____

_____

_____

2. Why is it harder to focus on improving your own effort and execution of your sales presentation than it is to complain about the circumstances affecting your success?

_____

_____

_____

_____

_____

_____

_____

3. If you consistently executed this process every day and focus on your effort and self-improvement, rather than on your circumstances, how many sales would this dare earn you over the next year? Circle one:

1   2   3   4   5   6   7   8

EFFORT

Rate your effort level towards improving yourself today with this dare:

1   2   3   4   5   6   7   8   9   10

_____

1: Did not read or do the dare. 2: Read the dare, but did not do it. 5. Did the dare with minimal effort. 10: Did the dare with 100% effort.

_**It's not just what you say,
but how you say it that counts.**_

DARE 14

More Than Words

READ

Your prospect's eyes light up when you show her the sports car of her dreams. What's more, today only, you have special pricing for new clients. You're in sales, so this is where you earn your keep. You must instill a sense of urgency in your buyer. She needs to truly understand, not just hear, that if she walks away, she'll miss a great opportunity.

It's a strong message and you're going to need a lot more than words to deliver it. According to Albert Mehrabian, psychology professor at UCLA, the combination of your tone of voice and body language account for 93 percent of the listener's interpretation of your message. That's thirteen times more influential than the words you say. Your words only account for 7 percent of how your message is received. Lesson learned: It's not just what you say, but *how* you say it that counts.

As Pete Townshend, guitarist and songwriter for the band The Who, says, "It's the singer, not the song that makes the music move along." No matter how powerful the message you're sharing (the song), you (the singer), must bring it to life.

HOW CAN I BRING MY MESSAGE TO LIFE?

THINK

Do you believe that 93 percent of how people interpret your message is based upon everything but the actual words you say? Why? Give an example of being "misinterpreted."

DARE

I dare you to focus your attention on your tone of voice and body language in your sales presentations. In between customer visits, practice by saying aloud, "The reason people choose us is..." Record yourself and play it back. Do you sound enthusiastic? Is the message believable? Ask your friends and family how you sound to them.

REFLECT

1. Would your friends and family say you sound enthusiastic and passionate when you talk about your products? Why or why not?

_____

_____

_____

_____

_____

_____

_____

_____

_____

2. Name three people you feel are persuasive because of their tone of voice and body language.

_____

_____

_____

3. How does their method compare to how you communicate?

_____

_____

_____

_____

_____

_____

_____

4. How will this information change how you communicate with your prospects?

_____

_____

_____

_____

_____

_____

_____

_____

5. How do you feel it affected your message to your customers?

_____

_____

_____

_____

_____

_____

_____

_____

6. What can you do in the future to remind yourself to focus on your tone of voice and body language in your communication with others?

_____

_____

_____

_____

_____

_____

_____

_____

7. If you consistently executed this process with every prospect you see over the next year, how many sales would this dare earn you?

1   2   3   4   5   6   7   8

DARE 14: MORE THAN WORDS

EFFORT

Rate your effort level towards improving yourself today with this dare:

1   2   3   4   5   6   7   8   9   10

_____

1: Did not read or do the dare. 2: Read the dare, but did not do it. 5. Did the dare with minimal effort. 10: Did the dare with 100% effort.

PAUSE HERE!

WEEK 2 SUMMARY

B efore you continue in your journey towards improvement, take a moment to get your bearings by completing your Week 2 Summary. **You must do this before you continue to Week 3.**

Average Effort Score for Week 2:

Review your Effort Scores from dares 8-14, and calculate your Average Effort Score for Week 2. Write it in the space below.

_____

4 or less = It's time to get serious. Recommit yourself to the program, and start fresh in Week 3 by striving for a 5 or higher each day!

5 to 7 = You're doing well, but you can do even better! Make a commitment today to raise the bar for yourself in Week 3, and strive for an average of 8 or better.

8 to 9 = What a great week! Keep pushing forward, and make it your personal goal to score all 9's and 10's in Week 3.

10 = Excellent! You are a rock star. If you maintain this effort level, you will receive the full benefit from this book.

What's it worth?

What was this week worth to you? Flip back through Week 2, and tally the number of sales that you said dares 8-14 would earn you. Write it below.

_____

14 dares down...26 to go!
You can do it!

WEEK THREE

Dares 15–21

DAY-ON DARES

____15. Mutual Accomplishment

____16. Gambling Is Prohibited on the Premises

____17. Start with a Purpose

____18. Get Ahead of the Pack

____19. One Simple Close

DAY-OFF DARES

____20. What Drives You?

____21. Focus on the "Just Looking" Buyer

"Selling is all about decisions."
—*Leadership Selling*

DARE 15

Mutual Accomplishment

READ

A mutual accomplishment occurs when two things happen: You succeed in creating urgency in your customer, **and** your customer makes an emotional commitment through verbal agreement. That verbal part is important. Mutual accomplishment cannot be achieved with just a nod of the head. The best way to secure such an agreement is to ask a solid closing question that allows the customer to eliminate all other choices in their mind and make a final decision.

While you may feel that you have created urgency, it's not a mutual accomplishment until you've secured outward agreement from the customer. Julie, a sales pro, helped demonstrate this point on one of our coaching calls. She was convinced that a customer was 100% in the bag, but couldn't tell me why except that he said he liked her product. I pushed a little more and asked why he liked hers more than the competition's. She still didn't know, so I asked Julie if it was possible that the customer told the competition the same thing. She admitted that was a possibility and recounted times when prospects told her the same thing and then ended up buying from someone else. What Julie needed to do was remove all the guesswork by asking mutual accomplishment questions.

Here's an example of a mutual accomplishment question:

"You said that of all the cars that I showed you, the four-door sedan was the best fit for you. Before you started looking at our products, you said that the minivan over at [competitor] was your favorite. Between ours and theirs, which one is better suited for your family's needs?"

If the customer says your product, then say, "I am always curious how my customers end up choosing their favorite product. So tell me, why do you feel this plan is a better fit?" On the other hand, if they tell you the competitor's car is still their favorite, then ask why and see if you can find a better product in your inventory.

The purpose of a mutual accomplishment question is to bring verbal resolution to the major decisions in their purchase. Remember, this is something you are doing *for* your customers, not *to* them. It helps them move forward in finding the best product, and it helps you eliminate guesswork.

Note: For further study on this topic, refer to Chapter 5 in my book *Creating Urgency*.

THINK

What is your biggest fear about asking the mutual accomplishment questions in the above script?

DARE

I dare you to ask the mutual accomplishment question below to every customer you see today. Practice the question aloud between customer visits to increase your comfort.

DARE 15: MUTUAL ACCOMPLISHMENT

"You said that of all the products that I showed you, our _____ was the best fit for you. Before you started looking here, you said that the (competitor's product) was your favorite. Between these two, which is better suited for your family's needs?"

REFLECT

1. Write out one example of a customer who you thought liked your product, but ended up buying from the competition.

_____

_____

_____

_____

_____

_____

_____

_____

_____

_____

_____

_____

_____

_____

THIS IS SOMETHING I DO
FOR MY CUSTOMERS
NOT TO THEM

2. Write out one example of a customer you practiced this process on today. Write the exact wording of your mutual accomplishment question as well as the customer's response.

_____

_____

_____

_____

_____

_____

_____

3. How will asking mutual accomplishment questions help you carry out the customer's mission of finding the best product?

_____

_____

_____

_____

_____

_____

_____

_____

4. If you consistently executed this process with every prospect you see over the next year, how many sales would this dare earn you? Circle one:

1   2   3   4   5   6   7   8

DARE 15: MUTUAL ACCOMPLISHMENT

EFFORT

Rate your effort level towards improving yourself today with this dare:

1   2   3   4   5   6   7   8   9   10

_____

1: Did not read or do the dare. 2: Read the dare, but did not do it. 5: Did the dare with half of my customers today. 10: Did the dare with all customers today, and rehearsed the questions between customer encounters.

"When it comes to building emotional urgency, your goal is to help the customer make a decision with confidence."
—*Creating Urgency*

DARE 16

Gambling Is Prohibited on the Premises

READ

*I*t's notoriously difficult to find a good stylist for curly hair, and my wife has some seriously curly hair. Shelly usually wears her brown curls long, but wanted to change it up a bit and have it cut just above her shoulders. She went to a new salon, met her hairdresser, and told her what she wanted. The hairdresser listened, said, "No problem," and started cutting away. Minutes into the cut, Shelly got nervous—it was much shorter than she had described. She told the stylist, but by this point, Shelly already had a pile of curly hair at her feet. Starting the cut before she understood what Shelly wanted was quite a gamble on the hairdresser's part. Shelly's confidence in the stylist faded fast, and the next half-hour was awkward and quiet for both of them.

Shelly left with zero faith in the stylist, and you had better believe she didn't go back.

All the hairdresser needed to do was summarize Shelly's vision back to her. This would have given the stylist the chance to make absolutely sure she understood Shelly's desired haircut, or to have Shelly clarify if necessary.

Shelly would have had confidence in the leadership of the hairstylist, and the stylist would have been sure that she was giving Shelly what she wanted.

In the same way, when a customer comes to look at your products, you must find out the general concept of what they are looking for and then summarize it back to them. This will increase your credibility with the customer, and it will give you confidence in the direction you should travel with them.

Save your gambling for the casino, not the dealership.

THINK

Why is it that people in sales positions, from those waiting tables to those selling big-ticket items, neglect to summarize back to the customer what the customer wants? Is it because of fear? Is it because they feel it's not necessary? How many communication blunders would be prevented if people would just restate what they heard a person say?

DARE

I dare you today to really listen to what the customer is looking for in their next vehicle. Once you understand what their vision of their new car is, summarize it back to them. Do not begin showing them a product until you can do this.

SUMMARIZE THE CUSTOMER'S VISION BACK TO THEM

REFLECT

1. Did you listen to each customer well enough to be able to summarize what they wanted? Explain.

_____

_____

_____

_____

_____

_____

2. Did you summarize the vision back to every customer you met today? If no, why not?

_____

_____

_____

_____

_____

3. How did summarizing the vision of the vehicle affect the demonstration? Did you find your sales process more purposeful?

_____

_____

_____

_____

_____

4. How did summarizing the vision affect your confidence in your solution for the customer?

_____

_____

_____

_____

_____

5. If you consistently executed this process with every prospect you see over the next year, how many sales would this dare earn you? Circle one:

1   2   3   4   5   6   7   8

EFFORT

Rate your effort level towards improving yourself today with this dare:

1   2   3   4   5   6   7   8   9   10

1: Did not read or do the dare. 2: Read the dare, but did not do it. 5: Did the dare with half of my customers today. 10: Did the dare with all customers today, and rehearsed the questions between customer encounters.

DARE 17

Start with a Purpose

READ

My tailor has a way of guiding me through the alteration process and assuring me that my suits are in good hands. He'll say things like, "Since you'd like the pant legs to fall a little higher on your shoes, I'm going to take the inseams in a little here." It's his way of letting me know he's heard me, and that he knows how to achieve my desired result. I leave feeling confident that I'm going to get a suit that fits just right.

As a sales pro, you're like that skilled tailor. No one knows the process, the end result, and the sales journey better than you do. You have to convey this confidence to your customers so they know where you are taking them, why you are leading in a specific direction, and how you will reach a successful end of the journey. You do this by giving the customer a ***purposeful transition statement***—it tells the buyer where you're heading and *why* you're going there. For you, the conversation might go like this:

"Based on your desire for plenty of cargo space, we'll look at our mid-size SUV. As you take your test drive, we'll talk about what's important to you, and by the end, I'll use everything you've told me to take you to the best product for your needs."

Like the tailor, you're assuring your customer that you heard their needs and know best how to meet them.

THINK

What will it say to the customer about you when you start off the sales presentation with a purposeful transition statement?

DARE

I dare you today to start off every sales presentation with a purposeful transition statement. Use the following template to help you, if you'd like.

"Based on your desire for _____ , we'll start with the _____. As you take your test drive, we'll talk about what's important to you, and by the end, I'll use everything you've told me to show you to the best vehicle for your needs."

REFLECT

1. What happened to your sales presentations today when you started off with a purposeful transition statement?

_____

_____

_____

_____

_____

_____

_____

2. How did it impact your confidence in showing the customer to the vehicle that best meets their needs?

_____

_____

_____

_____

_____

_____

3. If you consistently executed this process with every prospect you see over the next year, how many sales would this dare earn you? Circle one:

1   2   3   4   5   6   7   8

EFFORT

Rate your effort level towards improving yourself today with this dare:

1   2   3   4   5   6   7   8   9   10

_____

1: Did not read or do the dare. 2: Read the dare, but did not do it. 5: Did the dare with half of my customers today. 10: Did the dare with all customers today, and rehearsed the questions between customer encounters.

DARE 18

Get Ahead of the Pack

READ

1. How long have you been looking for a vehicle?
2. How many vehicles (including resale) have you seen?
3. If you had to choose a vehicle today, which one would it be?
4. Why is that your favorite product so far?

Picture yourself at the start of a four-leg relay race. Your palms are sweaty, your mouth is dry, and every muscle in your body is anticipating the familiar crack of the starting gun. Your competitors are lined up in the lanes to either side of you. They're ready, too. Now consider the four legs to be the four major factors that influence your customer's final decision: best product, best time frame, best price, and best manufacturer.

What would happen if you could start the race at the third leg while the other runners start at the first? You guessed it—you'd win the race! By asking the five simple questions listed at the beginning of this dare, you will uncover what matters most to your buyer, and you will zoom ahead of the pack. Now all you need to do is *listen* to their needs and find the product that has everything they love AND everything they haven't been able to find yet. It's a win/win. They get the product they've been looking for, you get the sale, and together you both cross the finish line. Everyone wins—except your competitors.

THINK

List the top three reasons you might resist (or have resisted) asking questions like the ones above. When you have your three reasons, consider this foolproof truth: Knowing what your clients want is better than not knowing, even if it's tough to hear. When you know the problem, you can work towards a solution.

DARE

I dare you today to focus on asking the five questions listed above within the first five minutes of meeting a new customer. Heck, try it with your old ones, too! Before the day starts and between each customer, say the five questions aloud so that you memorize them and feel comfortable using them.

REFLECT

1. How did using these questions feel? Explain.

_____

_____

_____

_____

_____

_____

_____

_____

2. With what percentage of your customers did you use all five questions?

_____%

Note: If the answer is 100%, then congratulate yourself for investing in your career, and move on to question 3. For anything less than 100%, consider why you didn't ask each question to each customer:

    a. It was uncomfortable.
    b. I was afraid of the answer.
    c. I forgot.
    d. I didn't want to.

3. What did you learn about your customers from using these questions?

_____

_____

_____

_____

_____

_____

_____

_____

_____

_____

_____

_____

IF I UNCOVER WHAT MATTERS MOST TO MY BUYER, I WILL ZOOM AHEAD OF THE PACK

<m

4. By asking these questions, were you better equipped to accomplish your customers' goals and, in so doing, to improve their lives? Explain.

_____

_____

_____

_____

_____

_____

_____

5. If you consistently executed this process with every prospect you see over the next year, how many sales would this dare earn you? Circle one:

1   2   3   4   5   6   7   8

EFFORT

Rate your effort level towards improving yourself today with this dare:

1 2 3 4 5 6 7 8 9 10

_____

1: Did not read or do the dare. 2: Read the dare, but did not do it. 5: Did the dare with half of my customers today. 10: Did the dare with all customers today, and rehearsed the questions between customer encounters.

DARE 19

One Simple Close

READ

Y ou won't need the mountains of books on how to close a deal if you can master just one technique. The most natural and effective tool I've found is the *summary close*, which leads into the *transaction close*. Check out the following summary:

"When we first started looking for your next vehicle, you said you were looking for a family-friendly car with plenty of cup holders and automatically-opening doors. While we were looking, you realized that you would enjoy a minivan more than a large SUV because it is more practical for your purposes. I showed you the ____, _____, and _____ , and you agreed that the minivan best fit what you were looking for. Well, Mr. and Mrs. Prospect, the only thing left for us to do is to get the paperwork started and write a deposit so that we can make this product yours! Are you ready to get started?"

Selling breaks down into three stages:
1. Understand the customer's mission.
2. Solve the customer's mission.
3. Hold the customer accountable to achieving their mission.

As in the scenario above, you summarize the first two stages (summary close), which sets you up to ask for the third stage (transaction close). Summarizing allows the customer to remember what they initially said they needed and then to agree that they made the decisions necessary to accomplish those needs. You keep the decision-making process moving forward by asking them to commit to the next step: the paperwork and the deposit.

Now that you've seen how a summary close leads naturally to a transaction close, it's time for you to practice using this strategy!

THINK

Do you believe the closing step is something you do *to* your prospects or *for* them? How does that belief affect your attitude and behaviors towards asking a final close question?

DARE

I dare you to use the summary close followed by the transaction close with every customer you talk to today. Practice between customer visits to increase your confidence with this new technique.

SUMMARY CLOSE → TRANSACTION CLOSE

REFLECT

1. What happened when you used the summary close followed by the transaction close today? Explain.

_____

_____

_____

_____

_____

_____

2. Regardless of whether the customer said yes or no, how did it feel using that closing strategy? Did it feel comfortable and natural? If not, then why not?

_____

_____

_____

_____

_____

3. Did summarizing the customer's stated needs and desires give you the confidence you needed to ask them to make the final purchase decision?

_____

_____

_____

_____

_____

4. If you consistently executed this process with every prospect you see over the next year, how many sales would this dare earn you? Circle one:

1 2 3 4 5 6 7 8

EFFORT

Rate your effort level towards improving yourself today with this dare:

1 2 3 4 5 6 7 8 9 10

1: Did not read or do the dare. 2: Read the dare, but did not do it. 5: Did the dare with half of my customers today. 10: Did the dare with all customers today, and rehearsed the questions between customer encounters.

WEEK 3

DAY-OFF DARES

---

*"Your desire to improve your own
life has more influence over your success
than any other factor."*

---

*"You have to change why you
sell before you can change how you sell."*

— *Creating Urgency*

DARE 20

What Drives You?

READ

P eople say I look like him, walk like him, and talk like him. But I got more from my dad than just looks. I got his independence and drive. When I was in high school, I asked him what career he'd recommend that would give me the most ownership over my results. I wanted to know that the harder I tried, the more I'd be rewarded. He advised me to go into commission sales and explained that sales professionals drive revenue for the entire company. Without them (without you), companies can't pay for any other staff member. Great sales professionals are in demand in every industry, in every city, and in every economy.

So let me ask you, why are you doing this? Why do you pound the pavement each day, work long and unpredictable hours, and live a less-convenient lifestyle than the 9-to-5ers? If your first thought was "to make money," then I challenge you to go a little deeper. What can the money bring you? Will it allow you to buy a home or car you've always desired? Will it help pay for your kid's college education? Will it bring you a better life?

Remember, the biggest advantage to being a sales professional is that you don't have to be dependent upon a certain salary. Yes, it's true that you risk making less than a salary-based job, but with greater risk, there's also a potential for greater reward.

So, what's your motivation? Humans are more emotional beings than they are logical. If you can tap into your emotional motivations and answer the questions in today's dare, you will be more successful.

THINK

Why did you choose a career in sales? Did you think it would be easy to make a lot of money, or were you excited that the harder you worked, the more money you'd make? In what ways has the career met or exceeded your expectations so far?

DARE

I dare you today to take an honest inventory of your motivations in the next section. How you answer these questions will impact how successful you can become.

REFLECT

1. What is your emotional motivation behind choosing a career in commission sales?

_____

_____

_____

_____

_____

_____

DARE 20: WHAT DRIVES YOU?

WHAT'S MY MOTIVATION?

2. On average, how much money do you make per sale? Note: Don't even think about writing a percent; you can't pay your mortgage with a percent.

$_____

3. How many cars do you need to sell each month to pay for your basic needs?

_____

4. How many cars do you need to sell each month to pay for your wants?

_____

5. How are you going to spend the money that you make above your needs? The more detail you write, the more you will mentally own this!

_____

_____

_____

_____

_____

_____

_____

_____

_____

_____

6. If you consistently focused on what money can do for you and your family, versus just working to sell a car, how many sales would this process earn you over the next year? Circle one:

1   2   3   4   5   6   7   8

EFFORT

Rate your effort level towards improving yourself today with this dare:

1   2   3   4   5   6   7   8   9   10

1: Did not read or do the dare. 2: Read the dare, but did not do it. 5. Did the dare with minimal effort. 10: Did the dare with 100% effort.

DAY OFF

DARE 21

Focus on the "Just Looking" Buyer

READ

*T*here are two types of buyers who walk onto your lot: those who admit to being buyers ("I'm looking for a sports car") and those who don't ("I just wanted to see what new technology there is"). I need you to focus on the second kind today.

Yes, I know. The cold, distant, closed-off customers are harder to sell to, but I want you to see every "just-looking, not-interested" buyer as a fun challenge. See how far you can take them in the sales process. Can you get them talking about their current vehicle/situation? Can you get them talking about the other products that they are "just looking" at? Can you get them to picture themselves behind the wheel of your latest arrival? It's not so much about selling them a vehicle, but about getting them to open up to you.

Remember that your distant little Looky Lous are sometimes actually buyers who just don't know how much they don't know. They're not even sure if they need a new car, and they certainly don't want to admit to themselves or to you that they're considering one. Nevertheless, something compelled them to start looking. They are on your lot after all.

By seeing each of these buyers as a challenge, you're making a way for yourself to become a better sales professional with all of your prospects, and you just might find a Looky Lou who wasn't "just looking," after all.

NEED TO SEE HOW FAR I CAN TAKE THEM IN THE SALES PROCESS

THINK

Write down a purchase that you have made in the past that started with an "I'm just looking" attitude. What made you go from "just looking" to signing on the dotted line?

DARE

I dare you this week to focus on the "just looking" buyers. Slow down and see how far you can take them in the sales process. Use any of the previous dares to help. Don't worry about selling them a car; just get them talking about their dissatisfaction with their current vehicle/situation.

REFLECT

1. Why are you so afraid of the "just looking" buyer? If you engage them, what's the worst thing that could happen? Explain.

_____

_____

_____

_____

_____

_____

2. How did your perception of "just looking" buyers change as you found out more about their dissatisfaction with their current situation?

_____

_____

_____

_____

_____

_____

3. What did you learn about yourself this week?

_____

_____

_____

_____

_____

_____

_____

_____

_____

_____

REMEMBER: SOMETHING COMPELLED THEM TO COME HERE

4. Write an example of how far you took a "just looking" buyer in the sales process this week. What did you do to get them to open up? Is there anything that you could have done to take the customer even further? If so, what?

_____

_____

_____

_____

_____

_____

_____

_____

_____

_____

_____

_____

_____

_____

_____

_____

_____

_____

_____

5. If you consistently executed this process with every closed-off prospect you see over the next year, how many sales would the strategy earn you? Circle one:

1   2   3   4   5   6   7   8

EFFORT

Rate your effort level towards improving yourself today with this dare:

1   2   3   4   5   6   7   8   9   10

—————————————

1: Did not read or do the dare. 2: Read the dare, but did not do it. 5. Did the dare with minimal effort. 10: Did the dare with 100% effort.

PAUSE HERE!

WEEK 3 SUMMARY

*B*efore you continue in your journey towards improvement, take a moment to get your bearings by completing your Week 3 Summary. **You must do this before you continue to Week 4.**

Average Effort Score for Week 3:

Review your Effort Scores from dares 15-21, and calculate your Average Effort Score for the week. Write it in the space below.

_____

4 or less = It's time to get serious. Recommit yourself to the program, and start fresh in Week 4 by striving for a 5 or higher each day!

5 to 7 = You're doing well, but you can do even better! Make a commitment today to raise the bar for yourself in Week 4, and strive for an average of 8 or better.

8 to 9 = What a great week! Keep pushing forward, and make it your personal goal to score all 9's and 10's in Week 4.

10 = Excellent! You are a rock star. If you maintain this effort level, you will receive the full benefit of this book.

What's it worth?

What was this week worth to you? Flip back through Week 3, and tally the number of sales that you said dares 15-21 would earn you. Write it below.

---

21 dares down...19 to go!
You can do it!

WEEK FOUR

Dares 22–28

DAY-ON DARES

DAY-OFF DARES

"People buy cars in every market. The only question is, from whom are they buying?"
— Creating Urgency

DARE 22

The Unsellable Sale

READD

O ne of my builder clients once had me analyze two communities with wildly different sales results for the same model. At one community, the plan simply wouldn't sell, but just 15 miles away, the same model was the top seller. Since buyer demographics, prices, and incentives were comparable in both neighborhoods, I went looking for the variable.

After a brief discussion with the sales professional at each location, I discovered the problem. The salesperson at the first community hated the layout and couldn't understand why anyone would want to buy this plan. However, in the second, the sales pro adored the plan and said that every customer he showed it to fell in love with the home. So what made the plan "unsellable"? The salesperson did. Scary, huh?

Whether you love or hate a product, you have to realize that it was designed specifically for *somebody*. By the time the plan reaches your dealership, it's already been through the ringer with hours of tweaks based on customer surveys, previous models, and research. Manufacturers know better than to throw a poor design out there and hope it works.

So get over yourself. Unless you're the one buying, it doesn't matter what you think. You're not going to live with it. Discover what's best for your customers, and you'll find that indeed, what you may call un-drivable is exactly what someone else wants to drive home.

THINK

How much are you letting your opinions about a particular product influence your message to your customers?

DARE

I dare you today to discover every hidden treasure about your least favorite product. Ask sales managers whom the manufacturer had in mind when they designed the car. What niche were they trying to fill? Call a previous buyer and ask what their favorite feature was. Find out what the car has that other plans lack.

Now, rewrite their answers into selling statements such as, "When the engineers designed this vehicle, they had _____ in mind." Or "People who choose this car are looking for...." Choose one of your selling statements, and share it with every prospect you see today.

REFLECT

1. What did you discover about your least favorite product today that you did not previously know?

_____

_____

_____

_____

2. Were you able to share your statements of why people choose that model with a customer today? If so, what happened?

_____

_____

_____

_____

_____

_____

3. How did creating the selling statement for your least favorite product change your opinion about that model?

_____

_____

_____

_____

_____

_____

4. What can you do in the future to not let your opinion get in the way of what is best for the customer?

_____

_____

_____

_____

_____

5. If you consistently executed this process with every prospect you see over the next year, how many sales would this dare earn you? Circle one:

1   2   3   4   5   6   7   8

EFFORT

Rate your effort level towards improving yourself today with this dare:

1   2   3   4   5   6   7   8   9   10

_____

1: Did not read or do the dare. 2: Read the dare, but did not do it. 5: Did the dare with half of my customers today. 10: Did the dare with all customers today, and rehearsed the questions between customer encounters.

"There are two types of sales professionals: those who participate in the sales process, and those who influence the sales process."
— *Creating Urgency*

DARE 23

"Let's Go Back to the Office"

READW

*T*here are many techniques to get a customer back into your office at the end of a sales presentation, but there are fewer techniques simpler than just telling them. My mother, a professor of speech, says, "Keep communication simple—tell people what you are going to tell them, tell them, and then tell them what you've told them."

So tell your customer up-front what to expect and how the process will go. You can say, "We're going to have a fun time together today. As we go through the products, I'll take notes on things that you like. Before you leave, we'll go back to the office and I will create a packet for you that summarizes everything we've seen today and what we've accomplished so far."

I want to encourage you to set this expectation as early as possible because the longer you wait, the more likely you are to chicken out.

Now let's fast-forward. You start out by telling them what to expect, you walk them through the models, and you take notes. When you're ready to take your customers back to the office, just lead the process by saying, "The next thing for us to do is head back to the office so that I can create a customized packet just for you. I can also look up the information on option pricing you were wondering about and write everything down for you."

Once they're in the sales office, summarize what you accomplished for them and answer any questions they have.

SET EXPECTATIONS AS EARLY AS POSSIBLE

I'm going to take some poetic license here and add a little something to Mom's advice: Tell them what you're going to tell them, tell them, tell them what you've told them. And then ask for the sale.

THINK

Why will you be more at ease when you tell your prospect early on that you'll be taking them back to your office?

DARE

I dare you today to use the technique above to get each customer back into your office at the end of the sales process. Between customer visits, practice saying the technique aloud to increase your confidence in executing this dare.

JUST TELL THEM

REFLECT

1. Why is it important to tell the buyer that you are going back to the office, versus asking them if they would like to go back? Explain.

_____

_____

_____

_____

_____

_____

2. What happened when you used this dare today? Explain.

_____

_____

_____

_____

3. What did your customers say when you told them that you would take them back to the sales office?

_____

_____

_____

_____

_____

4. If you consistently executed this process with every prospect you see over the next year, how many sales would this strategy earn you? Circle one:

1   2   3   4   5   6   7   8

EFFORT

Rate your effort level towards improving yourself today with this dare:

1   2   3   4   5   6   7   8   9   10

1: Did not read or do the dare. 2: Read the dare, but did not do it. 5: Did the dare with half of my customers today. 10: Did the dare with all customers today, and rehearsed the questions between customer encounters.

DARE 24

Create an Experience

READ

C UTCO, a company that specializes in high-end knives, doesn't sell its cutlery at Wal-Mart and Target. Instead, associates set up booths where customers can dice tomatoes effortlessly, cleanly trim the excess fat from chicken breasts, and slice through pennies with one squeeze of a pair of scissors. They don't just talk about their knives as tools of superior quality; they create an experience for their prospects. The customer will remember the CUTCO knife the next time they take an inferior blade to a tomato and struggle just to break the skin.

Similarly, creating an experience for your customers allows them to engage with the product and features rather than just viewing them from a distance. So take that extra step and let the kids sit in the minivan and watch a movie for a bit before they go home. Or take five extra minutes and encourage them to try the automatic opening doors. Don't limit the experiences to the obvious. Have them put their coffee cups and water bottles in the cup holders. Get creative. This helps your prospects appreciate the benefits, and it emotionally moves them toward the purchase.

Don't just point to a feature—give your customers an experience they'll want to recreate after they make the car theirs.

THINK

What happens when a customer's experience engages them in a product they are purchasing?

DARE

I dare you today to give each customer an experience centered on the features in your vehicles. To prepare, write out at least one feature for each of your top five sellers, and describe how you plan to experience those features with your customers.

REFLECT

1. What happened when you experientially engaged the customer in your vehicles today?

_____

_____

_____

_____

_____

_____

_____

_____

_____

2. What did you learn about your customers by helping them experience your features?

_____

_____

_____

_____

_____

_____

3. By engaging your customers in the experience, were you better equipped to accomplish your customers' goals and, in so doing, to improve their lives?

_____

_____

_____

_____

_____

_____

_____

_____

4. If you consistently executed this process with every prospect you see over the next year, how many sales would this dare earn you? Circle one:

1   2   3   4   5   6   7   8

EFFORT

Rate your effort level towards improving yourself today with this dare:

1   2   3   4   5   6   7   8   9   10

1: Did not read or do the dare. 2: Read the dare, but did not do it. 5: Did the dare with half of my customers today. 10: Did the dare with all customers today, and rehearsed the questions between customer encounters.

DARE 25

People Can't Argue with Emotion

READ

My mom (the speech professor and co-author of the public speaking textbook *Shared Meaning*) says, "When making an argument in a persuasive speech, make points that pull on people's heartstrings. Make your argument around emotion because people can't argue with emotion." The principles behind making a persuasive speech relate to the principles of selling.

Your customer can (and likely will) argue if you say, "Buy today because interest rates are going up," or "This promotion will only last three more days." However, they will have a much harder time arguing with you if you say, "Buy today because you said that your life would be less stressful if your kids could watch movies during long drives." In the latter, you're just letting your customers chew on the very thing they said was important: decreasing stress.

People are more likely to remember a persuasive speaker who tugs on their heartstrings than one who rattles off facts and figures. So, instead of closing your

CLOSE WITH EMOTION

sales presentation with interest rates, close it with images of stress-free family road trips or impressed coworkers. Trust me, people can't argue with emotion.

THINK

Think back to your last ten final arguments. Did you make your final arguments around emotion, or around logic? If you are leaning more towards logic, determine why you are discounting emotions.

DARE

I dare you today to make your final arguments to your customers based upon emotion and not logic. Practice between customer visits to increase your comfort and confidence with this new technique.

REFLECT

1. Were you comfortable or uncomfortable using this technique today? If you were uncomfortable, was it because you are not used to doing it, because you disagree with the concept, or for another reason? If you disagree, consider why.

_____

_____

_____

_____

_____

_____

_____

_____

2. Write out an example of how you used today's dare:

_____

_____

_____

_____

_____

_____

_____

_____

_____

_____

_____

_____

_____

_____

_____

_____

_____

_____

In the example you wrote above, consider the results and describe what happened, as well as what the customer said when you used today's dare.

3. If you consistently executed this process with every prospect you see over the next year, how many sales would this dare earn you? Circle one:

1   2   3   4   5   6   7   8

EFFORT

Rate your effort level towards improving yourself today with this dare:

1   2   3   4   5   6   7   8   9   10

1: Did not read or do the dare. 2: Read the dare, but did not do it. 5: Did the dare with half of my customers today. 10: Did the dare with all customers today, and rehearsed the questions between customer encounters.

DARE 26

Three Simple Phrases

READMENT

READ

I was watching a secret video shop of a sales professional who said three phrases that made certain she accomplished the customer's mission. The sentences started with:

- "You mentioned..."
- "How would this [feature] work for you?"
- and "Why?"

In her case (as a new home sales professional), it went like this: "You mentioned you needed a space for your grand piano. How and why would this space work for you?" These phrases are so simple, yet so powerful.

First, she showed that she was actively listening by bringing the piano back up after the customer had mentioned it. Second, she held him accountable to making a decision that accomplished one of his particular goals. Third, she got the customer involved emotionally in the decision by having him tell her why it would work.

Remember, selling is all about decisions. It is your job to take ownership of those decisions. Customers come in with a list of expectations that must be met for them to feel good about buying a car. When you facilitate faster decision-making, you increase the probability that they'll choose to buy their next vehicle from you.

TAKE OWNERSHIP: FACILITATE DECISION-MAKING

THINK

How do you view your role in the customer's decision-making process? Do you perceive yourself as a leader who works to speed up the process? Or, do you see yourself as someone who is there only when the customer has questions or concerns?

DARE

I dare you today to actively listen to your customers so you can understand all the decisions they need to make before purchasing from you. Then, use these simple yet powerful phrases:

- "You mentioned..."
- "How would this (_____) work for you?"
- and "Why does it work for you (or not work for you)?"

Do this with every customer you speak to today, and practice the technique between customer visits.

REFLECT

1. What happened when you actively listened to your customers today? How did it prepare you for the sales presentation?

_____

_____

_____

_____

_____

_____

2. What happened when you used the three phrases, "You mentioned...," "How does this _____ work?" and "Why does it work/not work for you?"

_____

_____

_____

_____

_____

3. By using those three phrases, how were you able to take the leadership role in the decision-making process?

_____

_____

_____

_____

_____

4. If you consistently executed this process with every prospect you see over the next year, how many sales would this dare earn you? Circle one:

1   2   3   4   5   6   7   8

EFFORT

Rate your effort level towards improving yourself today with this dare:

1   2   3   4   5   6   7   8   9   10

———————————

1: Did not read or do the dare. 2: Read the dare, but did not do it. 5: Did the dare with half of my customers today. 10: Did the dare with all customers today, and rehearsed the questions between customer encounters.

WEEK 4

DAY-OFF DARES

You cannot wait for buyers to walk in the door with their checkbooks out. You must create a sense of urgency for them.

DAY OFF

DARE 27

Don't Wait For Urgency
—Create It

READ

My wife and I were Christmas shopping when a sales professional approached and asked, "Can I show you something amazing?" I wasn't interested, but my wife said yes, so we went along. The sales professional asked Shelly and me to open our hands palm up, and then she dropped a dollop of sea salt scrub onto them. While we were rubbing the scrub over our hands, she asked what we did for a living. Since I am in sales, she wanted to know how often I shook people's hands. We continued the discussion as she poured a pitcher of water over our hands. After we'd washed off the scrub, she threw a towel over my hands, patted them dry and asked, "So how do they feel?" They felt good, as it turned out—very smooth. She turned to Shelly and asked, "Do you think the people who shake hands with your husband every day would be impressed if his hands felt like this?" I looked at Shelly, and then back at the sales pro. "We'll take two."

This sales professional created an experience that made me think about what my hands felt like to customers. So even though I wasn't going to the mall for sea salt scrub, I left with two jars: one for the office and one for home.

As a sales professional, you cannot wait for buyers to walk in the door with their checkbooks out. You must create a sense of urgency for them. Just like my sea salt scrub guru, you must learn to turn a "no" into a "yes."

THINK

Are you a sales professional who believes that customers will come to see you with urgency, or do you believe that it is your sole purpose to create urgency within your customers?

DARE

I dare you to go to your nearby mall today and study sales professionals. Take note of the people who create urgency, and compare them to the ones who wait for customers to come to them. What's different in the manner of these salespeople? How do they successfully create urgency? What are they doing that the other salespeople are not doing?

REFLECT

1. What are the traits of the sales professionals who created urgency?

_____

_____

_____

_____

_____

_____

_____

2. What are the traits of the salespeople who waited for people to come in with urgency?

_____

_____

_____

_____

_____

3. What did you learn about your own sales presentation?

_____

_____

_____

_____

_____

4. What do you plan on doing differently, starting this week?

_____

_____

_____

_____

_____

5. If you consistently took ownership over creating urgency with every prospect you see in the coming year, how many sales would this dare earn you?

1　2　3　4　5　6　7　8

EFFORT

Rate your effort level towards improving yourself today with this dare:

1   2   3   4   5   6   7   8   9   10

———————————————

1: Did not read or do the dare. 2: Read the dare, but did not do it. 5. Did the dare with minimal effort. 10: Did the dare with 100% effort.

DARE 28

Spend the Time

READ

Y ou've heard the saying, "It's quality that matters, not quantity." A sales professional I know from Phoenix decided to test the theory in relation to how much time he spent with his prospects. He told his sales partner that she could have all the new customers who came in while he was with his existing clients. Further, with more than forty new visitors per week, he wanted only ten. His goal was to take those ten as far in the sales process as he could and spend the rest of his time nurturing and following up with the buyers already in his pipeline.

His strategy was to slow down and focus on one buyer at time. He didn't jeopardize the relationship by trying to qualify them too early; he just focused on understanding the customers' mission to improve their lives. He worked *for* his prospects, dutifully searching out the best product and solving their mission. He didn't worry about the customers he might be missing. He focused on performing perfectly with each buyer and kept a journal of how he did, what mistakes he made, and what he could learn from those mistakes. In addition to improving his performance with each individual customer, he also found that he got more satisfaction out of getting to know his buyers and solving their problems.

I know, I know. What you really want to know is if the risk worked. Well, in two months, she consistently had *four times* as much traffic, but he had *twice as many sales*. In the end, our little risk taker had doubled his yearly income! Yeah, I'd say it worked, and that's why I'll sing the praises of "quality, not quantity" to all who will listen.

THINK

What is your biggest fear about focusing on one customer and taking them as far as you can in the sales process? Do you think it's possible that by slowing down and focusing on quality, you might sell more?

DARE

I dare you this week to focus on just one customer at a time, taking them as far as you can in the sales process. Do not worry about who you might be missing, but instead focus on what you are accomplishing with that one buyer.

REFLECT

1. Which of the following scenarios do you believe will give you a higher probability of selling more? Circle one:

   • 90 minutes per customer with 10 customers per week

   • 30 minutes per customer with 30 customers per week

SLOW DOWN AND FOCUS ON ONE BUYER AT A TIME

2. What would happen if you focused on taking just one customer at a time as far as you could in the sales process? How would your prospects feel if you were constantly engaged and without distraction?

_____

_____

_____

_____

_____

_____

_____

_____

_____

_____

_____

_____

_____

_____

_____

3. If you consistently executed this process with every prospect you see over the next year, how many sales would the strategy earn you? Circle one:

1   2   3   4   5   6   7   8

EFFORT

Rate your effort level towards improving yourself today with this dare:

1 2 3 4 5 6 7 8 9 10

_____

1: Did not read or do the dare. 2: Read the dare, but did not do it. 5. Did the dare with minimal effort. 10: Did the dare with 100% effort.

WEEK 4 SUMMARY

*B*efore you continue in your journey towards improvement, take a moment to get your bearings by completing your Week 4 Summary. **You must do this before you continue to Week 5.**

Average Effort Score for Week 4:

Review your Effort Scores from dares 22-28, and calculate your Average Effort Score for the week. Write it in the space below.

4 or less = It's time to get serious. Recommit yourself to the program, and start fresh in Week 5 by striving for a 5 or higher each day!

5 to 7 = You're doing well, but you can do even better! Make a commitment today to raise the bar for yourself in Week 5, and strive for an average of 8 or better.

8 to 9 = What a great week! Keep pushing forward, and make it your personal goal to score all 9's and 10's in Week 5.

10 = Excellent! You are a rock star. If you maintain this effort level, you will receive the maximum benefit from this book.

What's it worth?

What was this week worth to you? Flip back through Week 4, and tally the number of sales that you said dares 22-28 would earn you. Write it below.

_____

28 dares down...just 12 to go!
You can do it!

WEEK FIVE

Dares 29-35

DAY-ON DARES

____29. What If They Say No?

____30. Paint the Need

____31. Force the Compromise

____32. You Tell Me

____33. Remove Ambiguity

DAY-OFF DARES

____34. Pressure vs. Stress

____35. Inspiration Comes from Within

You're just helping them make a decision that gets them one step closer to their goal.

DARE 29

What If They Say No?

READ

I n 2009, I conducted a study of 100 salespeople. I looked for unsuccessful habits, trends in behavior, and traits that led to success. Out of the 100 salespeople I observed, *only one* sales pro asked his customers for the sale twice during their visit.

Think about your own experiences. When have you ever purchased anything from a sales professional the first time they asked? If you are like most people, your reflexive response is, "No," but inside, the wheels start turning and you're considering whether you should or should not move forward with the purchase. That's when the real questions and concerns come up. If the sales professional would only continue the conversation and ask questions to uncover those concerns, you would probably realize that there is nothing to fear, and you might even end up purchasing the item you initially declined. This is also true of the customers you see every day.

You must look at asking for the sale as helping your customers achieve a resolution to their quest. They told you that your vehicle would improve their lives, so you're just helping them make a decision that gets them one step closer to *their* goal. When they say no to your first closing attempt, use that as a springboard to find out what's not quite right. You can say, "If we have found the vehicle that you said would be perfect for you and your family, then what are your concerns? Is there something that you are not happy with, or are you just uncomfortable moving forward on this big decision?"

If they admit their discomfort, then say, "I understand your fear. Buying a car is a big deal, but I feel confident that we've accomplished everything that you said you desired in your next vehicle. Do you feel that we have missed anything?"

If you have missed something, or if they bring up a hidden desire, then address it. On the other hand, if they agree that this is the best product, then say, "I will be here for you every step of the way and would be honored to have you as the newest member of our [dealership] family. What do you think?"

Even if they say no to your second attempt, they know that you really desire to have them buy from you. That's a great thing, and it will grant you a higher status in their minds than any other salesperson they meet. If they say yes (and many of them will), you have accomplished another sale.

THINK

If a customer believes your product is the best for them, do you feel that asking them to purchase twice in the same visit will hurt your chances of making a sale, or take you one step closer? Why?

ASKING FOR THE SALE LEADS MY CUSTOMERS **TO ACHIEVE A RESOLUTION**

DARE

I dare you today to ask every customer twice for the sale. Memorize and use the script above when a customer says no to your first closing attempt.

DARE 29: WHAT IF THEY SAY NO?

REFLECT

1. How did this process change your perception about asking for the sale twice during the same visit? Explain.

_____

_____

_____

_____

_____

_____

2. What happened when you used this dare today? What did you learn about the customer and yourself?

_____

_____

_____

_____

_____

_____

_____

3. If you consistently executed this process with every prospect you see over the next year, how many sales would this dare earn you? Circle one:

1   2   3   4   5   6   7   8

EFFORT

Rate your effort level towards improving yourself today with this dare:

1   2   3   4   5   6   7   8   9   10

_____

1: Did not read or do the dare. 2: Read the dare, but did not do it. 5: Did the dare with half of my customers today. 10: Did the dare with all customers today, and rehearsed the questions between customer encounters.

DARE 30

Paint the Need

READ

When the reward of a purchase outweighs the risks, people buy. Sometimes people think a new car might be nice, but they aren't urgent because their current desires don't outweigh the prospect of taking on a higher monthly payment or cutting their savings account in half. This is when you have to paint the need.

So first you use all those earlier dares that discuss how to find out exactly what they're looking for in a car. If there aren't enough admitted desires to justify the cost of ownership, then you have to paint the need to create new desires.

You can do that by educating them on needs they didn't realize. My biggest example is of a sales professional who cured a disease I didn't even know I could be rid of: butt sweat. I never would have entered a dealership and said, "I need a cure for butt sweat" because I didn't even know that air conditioned seats existed. But this sales pro painted the need (and got the sale, by the way).

There are plenty of things that your car has that your customers don't even know they need. For me, it was a cure for butt sweat. For a busy parent, it might be a setup that allows them to get to the third row without taking the car seats out. They may not even know that's possible, but when you illuminate them, they realize they just *have* to have it.

The goal is to find a car that improves their life enough that the reward outweighs the risk.

Reward > cost of waiting + monthly payment + down payment

Do your part to make the purchase justifiable in the customer's mind.

REWARD MUST OUTWEIGH RISK

THINK

How would it benefit your customers if you presented solutions to problems they didn't even know they had?

DARE

I dare you today to make a list of all the little-known features and the benefits they provide to would-be buyers.

REFLECT

1. Did you present solutions to problems your clients didn't realize they had? Circle one: YES   NO

Note: If you did, then congratulate yourself for investing in your career, and move on to question 2. If not, consider why you didn't present solutions to your customers:

a. It was uncomfortable.
b. I was afraid.
c. I forgot.
d. I didn't want to.

2. What did you learn about your prospects through this process?

_____

_____

_____

_____

_____

3. If you consistently executed this process with every prospect you see over the next year, how many sales would this strategy earn you? Circle one:

1   2   3   4   5   6   7   8

EFFORT

Rate your effort level towards improving yourself today with this dare:

1   2   3   4   5   6   7   8   9   10

1: Did not read or do the dare. 2: Read the dare, but did not do it. 5: Did the dare with half of my customers today. 10: Did the dare with all customers today, and rehearsed the questions between customer encounters.

DARE 31

Force the Compromise

READ

W hen dancers are in sync, one partner leads and the other follows. There is an emotional connection that goes beyond memorizing the steps. The result is a fluid movement that appears effortless. It's magic.

The magic is lost, though, when partners lose their connection, and thus, the rhythm of the dance. They focus too much on the nuts and bolts of the technique, and they start looking at their feet instead of their partner's eyes.

Demonstrating a vehicle can be a lot like a dance. When you're in your groove, it's fun for you and for your customer. You follow each other's cues. It's natural and unforced. On the other hand, when it feels forced or even manipulated, demonstrating the product can be uncomfortable and tense.

One of the easiest ways to lose your selling rhythm is to get bogged down in details of everything that could possibly be added to the car. This is like looking down at your feet during a dance. You lose the emotional connection with the buyer, and thus the opportunity to engage them in the product on a personal level.

You do need to find out what's important to them—what options they have to have and which ones they can do without. To keep your rhythm, never be afraid to force the compromise. You're still looking for the little black dress that is closest to what they're looking for. So stay in control and lead your prospects to their little black dress.

Here's a hint: As the sales professional, you're the leader. Think about it. You know your products better than anyone else, so take a proactive approach. Before opening the door to the first vehicle, say, "In each of our products, we showcase both the included features and the optional features so that you can see our flexibility in tailoring the vehicle to meet your unique taste. While we go through the demonstration, if you are interested in a particular feature you see, let me know and I will put it on your wish list. Then at the end, I will go back and create a master list of all the options that caught your eye, along with their prices."

This lets you maintain the emotional connection with your customer. Dancing is more fun for everyone when you're not looking at your feet.

THINK

The selling rhythm allows you to remain in control of the experience. It also gives you a specific reason to sit down with your client at the end of the presentation and review their wish list. List two of your own reasons for why the selling rhythm is so important.

DARE

I dare you today to proactively tell each customer about creating a wish list. Don't worry about creating your own version of the script, but instead just memorize the one given to you above. Once you get comfortable using the script, then you can make it your own.

> ONE OF THE EASIEST WAYS TO LOSE MY SELLING RHYTHM IS TO GET BOGGED DOWN IN THE "STANDARD VS. OPTIONAL" DISCUSSION

REFLECT

1. How did using the script feel?

_____

_____

_____

_____

_____

2. With what percentage of your customers did you use the script?

_____%

Note: If the answer is 100%, then congratulate yourself for investing in your career and move on to question 3. For anything less than 100%, consider why you didn't use the script with each customer:

  a. It was uncomfortable.
  b. I was afraid of the answer.
  c. I forgot.
  d. I didn't want to.

3. Were you able to stay in control of the customer presentation, or did you get stuck in the "standard vs. optional" trap? Explain.

_____

_____

_____

_____

_____

4. Did you use the wish list as a reason to sit down with the customer at the very end of the presentation? Explain.

_____

_____

_____

_____

_____

_____

_____

5. If you consistently executed this process with every prospect you see over the next year, how many sales would this dare earn you? Circle one:

1   2   3   4   5   6   7   8

EFFORT

Rate your effort level towards improving yourself today with this dare:

1   2   3   4   5   6   7   8   9   10

1: Did not read or do the dare. 2: Read the dare, but did not do it. 5: Did the dare with half of my customers today. 10: Did the dare with all customers today, and rehearsed the questions between customer encounters.

Let your customer tell you their own solution.

DARE 32

You Tell Me

READ

"You tell me" is one of the most powerful phrases that you can use to handle customer concerns. I recently watched a new home sales professional use this strategy successfully for three objections in a row. In one, the customer felt the kitchen was too dark. The sales pro said, "Okay, well, you tell me how you would fix it?" The customer described how the lighting in the adjacent room would help and how she could add under-cabinet lights and a lamp. It was amazing. Without providing a solution and with only three words, the sales professional solved the objection.

Maybe they had their mind set on having power seats or in-car navigation.

So you say, "Okay, you tell me what you're thinking about this and about the overall car."

Often, your prospect will say something like, "Well, how often do you really move your seats?" or "Oh, I guess I can just keep using my phone for navigation.

It's easier to use anyway."

When you say to a customer, "You tell me," one of two things will happen: Either 1) your customer will come up with their own solution, or 2) you'll buy yourself some time to come up with an adequate answer. Either way, you are better off holding your tongue and saying, "You tell me."

THINK

Do you feel that you always have to be the one to come up with the solution? If so, why? In the last week, for which objections could your customers have created their own solutions?

DARE

I dare you today to say, "You tell me what you would do," when your customers have objections.

REFLECT

1. Write out a specific example of an objection that you used this technique on today.

_____

_____

_____

_____

_____

_____

_____

2. What happened?

_____

_____

_____

_____

_____

3. How will using "you tell me" benefit you with future objections?

_____

_____

_____

_____

4. If you consistently executed this process with every prospect you see over the next year, how many sales would this dare earn you? Circle one:

1   2   3   4   5   6   7   8

EFFORT

Rate your effort level towards improving yourself today with this dare:

1   2   3   4   5   6   7   8   9   10

1: Did not read or do the dare. 2: Read the dare, but did not do it. 5: Did the dare with half of my customers today. 10: Did the dare with all customers today, and rehearsed the questions between customer encounters.

Your customers will appreciate that you took the time to explain what's unique about the product they're considering calling their own.

DARE 33

Remove Ambiguity

READ

T here's nothing more discouraging than spending all day surveying a million potential gifts but getting no closer to finding the perfect one for someone. That's about the time it starts to seem like a good idea to get your wife a blender or a vacuum cleaner.

When the choices are vast and the decisions are too numerous, it causes ambiguity, which drives people to make poor decisions, delay decisions altogether, or mentally check out. The problem is that sales pros often contribute to the problem and make prospects feel even further from a solution than when they started.

It's easy to get lost in the details when buying a car. Your customer's got to think about color, make, manufacturer, options, and upgrades. It can be crippling! As a sales pro, you must narrow the decision and remove ambiguity.

Facilitate victories by accomplishing each step one at a time. The customer shouldn't feel like you're forcing them to buy from you, but you can put pressure on moving them toward a decision and clearing up ambiguity. Watch your language, though. Say, "Which would you prefer?" rather than, "Think it over and let me know."

Praise your buyers for each decision accomplished along the way before moving on to the next. Be a part of the solution. Help eliminate ambiguity so that your prospects don't quit before they even have a chance to start.

THINK

Have you ever felt so overwhelmed by a buying process that even though you want to move forward, you just delay the decision instead?

DARE

I dare you to use questions that eliminate ambiguity and move the prospect forward.

REFLECT

1. What do you think is the biggest benefit to your customers of removing ambiguity during the purchasing process?

_____

_____

_____

_____

_____

_____

_____

_____

DARE 33: REMOVE AMBIGUITY

2. In what ways did removing ambiguity take pressure off of your buyers?

_____

_____

_____

_____

_____

3. Did you notice visible relief from any of your prospects as you facilitated their forward progress?

_____

_____

_____

_____

4. If you consistently executed this process with every prospect you see over the next year, how many sales would this dare earn you? Circle one:

1   2   3   4   5   6   7   8

EFFORT

Rate your effort level towards improving yourself today with this dare:

1   2   3   4   5   6   7   8   9   10

_____

1: Did not read or do the dare. 2: Read the dare, but did not do it. 5: Did the dare with half of my customers today. 10: Did the dare with all customers today, and rehearsed the questions between customer encounters.

WEEK 5

DAY-OFF DARES

When we've done everything in our power to succeed, we might feel pressure, but not stress.

DARE 34

Pressure vs. Stress

READ

As an alumni advisor for my fraternity, I hear about final exam week every year. Inevitably, I remember my own college days and how I handled (and sometimes did not handle) final exam week. Sometimes I spent the month before exams hanging out with my friends and watching TV. Then on the night before the exam, I drank gallons of coffee and crammed. I'd approach the test exhausted, uncertain, and stressed beyond belief because I had not prepared. Other times though, I'd spend the month before the exam in the library or at my desk—books open and mind focused. I'd review my notes on the night before and then go to bed early. I'd wake up prepared and confident. Would I feel some pressure to do a great job? Sure I would, but I would not feel stress. I would take the test with confidence because I knew I had prepared.

The problem for many of us is that when we have "final exams," such as making our sales numbers, we feel stressed and uncertain. The difference, though, is when we've done everything in our power to succeed, we might feel pressure, but not stress.

Remember, in work as in life, we are measured not by our failures, but by our ability to look our failures in the eye and come back faster, stronger, and better.

What objections are you struggling with that you must learn to overcome? Which stages of the sales process are these objections bringing to a halt? What can you do, or learn to do, in order to keep the sale moving forward at that stage?

At the end of each day, ask yourself if you accomplished all your action points for that day.

THINK

Do you feel pressure or stress to make your sales goals this month? If you feel stress, write down three things you can do to be better prepared.

DARE

I dare you today to write out daily goals for the next week. At the beginning of each day, remind yourself of what you must accomplish on that day to get closer to reaching your income goal.

REFLECT

1. Write down your success strategy to achieve your sales goals during the next thirty days. The success strategy should include what you believe are the everyday behaviors that you should do to give yourself the highest probability of reaching your income goal.

_____

_____

_____

_____

_____

2. If you consistently executed this process every day over the next year, how many sales would this dare earn you? Circle one:

1   2   3   4   5   6   7   8

EFFORT

Rate your effort level towards improving yourself today with this dare:

1   2   3   4   5   6   7   8   9   10

———————————————

1: Did not read or do the dare. 2: Read the dare, but did not do it. 5. Did the dare with minimal effort. 10: Did the dare with 100% effort.

Daily incentives provide:

1) instant gratification
2) opportunity for accountability

DAY OFF

DARE 35

Inspiration Comes from Within

READ

I started my sales career selling homes in a community with a nine-month build cycle and no inventory. No inventory means no quick money, and a nine-month build cycle means a long wait for that first check. I was excited to eventually break even on my draw and then to exceed it, but I needed daily motivation for the big money in the distance. And I needed someone to hold me accountable.

For me, that someone was my wife. Shelly and I agreed that every time I took a contract to start building a home, I could buy a custom-made shirt. This gave me daily incentive by providing instant gratification, and it allowed her to hold me accountable. Every night she'd ask, "Were you able to buy a new shirt tonight?" The $75 I spent on each shirt was no big deal—it was just a short-term investment towards the commission ahead. I was younger then, so my priorities were different, but the principle remains. The "instant gratification" strategy kept me focused on what I needed to do to be successful.

Motivation is something that's given to you (pep talks, incentives, contests, etc). Inspiration comes from within—your own motivation to achieve something. Find something to keep you inspired to pound the pavement every day.

THINK

Are you going at this alone? Who is one person you can call today to help keep you accountable for your success?

DARE

I dare you today to ask at least one person to be part of your support group. Tell them what you are doing and how they can help you by holding you accountable. Come up with an immediate gratification reward.

REFLECT

1. Who can be in your support group?

_____

_____

_____

_____

2. Write out what you are going to ask them to do in order to keep you accountable.

_____

_____

_____

_____

_____

_____

3. How often would you like them to contact you to ask the accountability question?

_____

4. Write down an immediate gratification reward—something you can buy yourself or do for yourself every time you sell a product.

_____

_____

5. If you consistently focused on an immediate gratification reward and had a support person hold you accountable, how many sales would this dare earn you over the next year? Circle one.

1   2   3   4   5   6   7   8

EFFORT

Rate your effort level towards improving yourself today with this dare:

1   2   3   4   5   6   7   8   9   10

_____

1: Did not read or do the dare. 2: Read the dare, but did not do it. 5. Did the dare with minimal effort. 10: Did the dare with 100% effort.

PAUSE HERE!

WEEK 5 SUMMARY

Before you continue in your journey towards improvement, take a moment to get your bearings by completing your Week 5 Summary. **You must do this before you continue to Week 6.**

Average Effort Score for Week 5:

Review your Effort Scores from dares 29-35, and calculate your Average Effort Score for the week. Write it in the space below.

---

4 or less = It's time to get serious. Recommit yourself to the program, and start fresh in Week 6 by striving for a 5 or higher each day!

5 to 7 = You're doing well, but you can do even better! Make a commitment today to raise the bar for yourself in Week 6, and strive for an average of 8 or better.

8 to 9 = What a great week! Keep pushing forward, and make it your personal goal to score all 9's and 10's in Week 6.

10 = Excellent! You are a rock star. If you maintain this effort level, you will receive the maximum benefit from this book.

What's it worth?

What was this week worth to you? Flip back through Week 5, and tally the number of sales that you said dares 29-35 would earn you. Write it below.

_____

35 dares down...only 5 to go!
You can do it!

WEEK SIX

Dares 36-40

DAY-ON DARES

_____36. Selling the Intangible

_____37. One-Hour Follow-Up

_____38. Give Them an Assignment

DAY-OFF DARES

_____39. Effort or Ability?

_____40. Stump Me Twice, Shame on Me

---

*You must sell what your customers
are looking for: a better life.*

DARE 36

Selling the Intangible

READ

*S*tarbucks made the concept of the "third place" famous, but the idea isn't new. In the sitcom *Cheers,* Norm Peterson's "third place" is the namesake bar where everybody knows your name. It's that place of comfort, social interaction, and community that is neither the home nor the office.

When you are selling tangible benefits like road safety and fuel efficiency, you must sell what your customers are really looking for: a better life. This better life isn't just about a car; it's about the stress relief they'll get by having kids entertained in the backseat. It's about the peace of mind they'll feel knowing that they have a reliable vehicle and won't get stuck in the middle of Kansas while they're on family road trips. Don't just sell your prospects on a vehicle; sell them on the sense of pride or peace they'll have from their purchase.

THINK

In the following table, there are two columns and three rows. In the left column, you will write down at least three features that your manufacturer offers. In the right column, for each of those amenities, write at least one statement or question that you can use to get the customer thinking about the intangible aspects of the feature.

PRODUCT BENEFITS	STATEMENTS/ QUESTIONS
1.	
2.	
3.	

DARE

I dare you today to use at least one of your products' features with every customer you talk to. While you are demonstrating, use your intangible statements or questions to get the customer thinking emotionally.

REFLECT

1. How did using these questions or statements feel?

_____

_____

_____

_____

_____

2. With what percentage of your customers did you ask a question or use a statement?

_____%

Note: If the answer is 100%, then congratulate yourself for investing in your career and move on to question 3. For anything less than 100%, consider why you didn't ask a question with each customer:

    a. It was uncomfortable.
    b. I was afraid of the answer.
    c. I forgot.
    d. I didn't want to.

3. What did you learn about your customers from using these statements and questions?

_____

_____

_____

_____

_____

4. By asking these questions, were you better equipped to accomplish your customers' goals and, in so doing, to improve their lives?

_____

_____

_____

_____

_____

5. If you consistently executed this process with every prospect you see over the next year, how many sales would this dare earn you? Circle one:

1   2   3   4   5   6   7   8

EFFORT

Rate your effort level towards improving yourself today with this dare:

1   2   3   4   5   6   7   8   9   10

―――――――――

1: Did not read or do the dare. 2: Read the dare, but did not do it. 5: Did the dare with half of my customers today. 10: Did the dare with all customers today, and rehearsed the questions between customer encounters.

---

*Your biggest competitor is the conversation
your customer will have about you and
your product once they leave.*

DARE 37

One-Hour Follow-Up

READ

W ho or what is your biggest competitor? Is it the market, the economy, or maybe the competing dealerships? While all of these factors play into your buyer's decision, the answer isn't in the list above. Your biggest competitor is the conversation your customer will have about you and your product once they leave.

On their way out the door (and down the street to the dealership around the corner), your customers are talking about you and thinking of several questions and concerns about your product. They're asking their significant other, "What about this?" and "What if that?" Chances are, they're not going to call you to find out the answers. They're just going to keep moving forward—right into one of your competitor's vehicles.

How do you combat this? *You* call them while all those questions and concerns are still fresh. This gives you the best opportunity to address all their questions and put their minds at ease. It also helps you establish your credibility as a professional who cares about his/her prospects.

So don't wait until next week when you "have a minute" to make those follow-up calls. *Create* the time today and get ready to create yourself a contract.

THINK

Write down a past experience when you were shopping for something, did not make a decision, had a question, but left without asking the salesperson. Don't you wish you would have asked your question while you were there? Now, what would have happened if the salesperson had called you and said, "Thanks for spending time with me today. Whenever I leave a store, I usually have a question that I wished I would have asked but forgot to. Did that happen to you? Do you have any additional questions that I could answer for you?"

DARE

I dare you today to call every one of your prospects within one hour after they walk out your door.

REFLECT

1. What happened when you called your prospects today?

_____

_____

_____

2. Write down one example of someone you called and the resulting conversation.

_____

_____

_____

_____

_____

3. Did it help or hurt your probability of moving the sale forward? Why?

_____

_____

_____

_____

_____

4. How do you feel your customers perceived you on the phone?

    a. "This sales professional really wants to help and make this process as easy as possible for us."

    b. Or "This salesperson is so pushy."

Which perception did you choose, and why?

_____

_____

_____

_____

_____

5. In the end, was calling your prospects within one hour worth doing? Why?

_____

_____

_____

_____

_____

6. If you consistently executed this process with every prospect you see over the next year, how many sales would this dare earn you? Circle one:

1   2   3   4   5   6   7   8

EFFORT

Rate your effort level towards improving yourself today with this dare:

1   2   3   4   5   6   7   8   9   10

———————————

1: Did not read or do the dare. 2: Read the dare, but did not do it. 5: Did the dare with half of my customers today. 10: Did the dare with all customers today, and rehearsed the questions between customer encounters.

---

*You want your customers to compare the
other dealerships to your standard, not the other
way around.*

DARE 38

Give Them an Assignment

READ

W hat do you do when your customers love your product, but simply won't commit? Well, you can demonstrate confidence in and help push them toward a decision with one simple act. Send them on their way with a personalized "dare to compare" sheet.

This is how it works. You get out a piece of paper and a red marker and say,

> "I understand that you want to look around. Since I have a strong sense of what you're looking for, I'd like to help make your search as easy as possible. Let's summarize what you need in your next vehicle."

While you restate what they've told you, write the items down. As you list their needs, focus on the areas that make your product different from your competition so that your customers will compare the other dealerships to *your* standard, not the other way around. When you're done say, "This should make your buying adventure easier, don't you think? More than anything, I hope you find the best product for you and your family. Good luck!"

If you don't see them within 24 hours, call and ask how the sheet is working for them. Ideally, they'll return to you with the paper in hand—red markings all over it. In this case, welcome them back and ask them how the list helped them in finding their next vehicle. Simply by returning, they're giving a strong signal that they want what you have to offer. So give it to them.

THINK

What does it say about your confidence in your product when you give your clients a personalized "dare to compare" sheet?

DARE

I dare you today to give every customer the personalized "dare to compare" sheet before they walk out your door. Note: This is not a standardized marketing sheet that every customer receives.

REFLECT

1. How did it feel to be able to create a personalized "dare to compare" sheet with your customers today? Did it give you a sense of accomplishment that you were able to take the customer as far as possible today?

_____

_____

_____

_____

_____

_____

_____

2. How will this technique help you in following up with your customers?

_____

_____

_____

_____

_____

_____

_____

3. How will creating a personalized "dare to compare" sheet give you a competitive advantage? What does it say about you in the minds of your customers?

_____

_____

_____

_____

_____

_____

_____

_____

_____

IF I DON'T HEAR FROM THEM WITHIN 24 HOURS, I NEED TO CALL AND ASK HOW THE SHEET IS **WORKING FOR THEM**

4. If you consistently executed this process with every prospect you see over the next year, how many sales would this dare earn you? Circle one:

1   2   3   4   5   6   7   8

EFFORT

Rate your effort level towards improving yourself today with this dare:

1   2   3   4   5   6   7   8   9   10

———————————

1: Did not read or do the dare. 2: Read the dare, but did not do it. 5: Did the dare with half of my customers today. 10: Did the dare with all customers today, and rehearsed the questions between customer encounters.

WEEK 6

DAY-OFF DARES

What sets an average salesperson apart
from an exceptional sales pro?

DAY OFF

DARE 39

Effort or Ability?

READ

“ *I*f a man is called to be a street sweeper, he should sweep streets even as Michelangelo painted, or Beethoven composed music, or Shakespeare wrote poetry. He should sweep streets so well that all the hosts of heaven and earth will pause to say, 'Here lived a great street sweeper who did his job well.'”

—Dr. Martin Luther King, Jr.

Congratulations, you're a salesperson. You wrote a resume that caught someone's eye, you demonstrated your professionalism in the interviews, and you passed the tests. The social skills that come naturally to you border upon painful to someone else. If you've made it this far, you have "the stuff." So what sets an average salesperson apart from an exceptional sales pro?

Dr. King's examples were prolific artists in their respective fields, but it's easy to take for granted the time they spent chiseling, composing, or writing and rewriting with quill in hand. You had better believe that as they fell asleep at night, Michelangelo visualized his next subject, Beethoven composed new melodies, and Shakespeare spun new plots.

The truth is, we never would have heard of Michelangelo if he hadn't expended an enormous amount of effort. He sculpted at least 42 major works in addition to his large body of paintings. Beethoven composed hundreds of pieces ranging from solos to full symphonies, and Shakespeare wrote more than 40 plays and enough poetry to fill volumes.

Often we look at the success of those at the top of their fields and dismiss it as unattainable. We use "they're special" or "I'll never be that good" as excuses to not spend the energy and time necessary to excel. How many more Michelangelos, Beethovens, and Shakespeares would we have if everyone put that much effort into their gifts?

THINK

How much more money would you have in the bank if you put that kind of effort into your trade?

DARE

I dare you to put forth the level of effort that Dr. King speaks of and to do that every day from this day forward. See what happens to your success.

REFLECT

1. In the table on the next page, there are two columns. In the left column, write down three activities/skills that you are good at (photography, video games, basketball, etc.). In the right column, write down how much time you spend thinking about or doing those activities on an average day.

DARE 39: EFFORT OR ABILITY

ACTIVITIES/SKILLS I'M GOOD AT	TIME SPENT
1.	
2.	
3.	

2. Now, in the left column below, write down three activities/skills that you admire in others but aren't so good at (public speaking, writing, math, study skills, etc.), and in the right column, write how much time you spend thinking about or doing these activities on an average day.

ACTIVITIES/SKILLS I'M NOT GOOD AT	TIME SPENT
1.	
2.	
3.	

3. What's the difference between the first group and the second group?

_____

_____

_____

_____

_____

_____

If you're like me, you spend more time on the first three activities. So, how can you become better at the items in the second group? What's the solution? Spend just as much time in the areas that you are not as good at as you do in the areas where you are skilled.

4. Over the next year, if you consistently invested as much effort into the areas where your skills are lacking as you would for the areas where you are skilled, how many sales would this dare earn you? Circle one:

1   2   3   4   5   6   7   8

EFFORT

Rate your effort level towards improving yourself today with this dare:

1   2   3   4   5   6   7   8   9   10

_____

1: Did not read or do the dare. 2: Read the dare, but did not do it. 5. Did the dare with minimal effort. 10: Did the dare with 100% effort.

DARE 40

Stump Me Twice, Shame on Me

READ

*H*ow would your interactions with customers change if you knew that you'd never hear an objection? In that lovely world, would you show that car with the bright orange paint job? Would you make your follow-up calls more frequently and fearlessly? Would you feel more confident? Let's face it, you're not going to be a very effective sales professional if you let fear of objections keep you from, well, from *selling*. This lesson is twofold. First, work as if you're not afraid of objections. Second, since you know that you will have objections, take ownership of your career by being as prepared as possible to address them. You should always have answers ready for the objections you can anticipate. But what about those stumpers that are bound to come your way? Those are your biggest opportunities to turn a no into a yes. When someone hands you a stumper, it's okay not to have an answer right then. Yes, I said it's okay... the *first time* (stump me once, shame on you). But it's not okay the second time (stump me twice, shame on me). So *find* answers. Look on the Internet, ask your sales manager, do whatever it takes—just make sure you do *something* so that the next time a customer has the same objection, it doesn't stump you.

In short: work as if you're not afraid of objections, but when you get one, don't let it stump you twice.

> "STUMPERS" ARE MY BIGGEST OPPORTUNITY TO TURN A **NO INTO A YES**

THINK

When was the last time your fear of objections limited your sales presentation? What would you have done differently if you hadn't had that fear?

DARE

I dare you today to write a list of all the objections that have stumped you in the past. Pick the three most frequent ones, and find a solution to each by the end of today. When you find the solution, say it aloud. This will increase your confidence as well as the probability that you'll remember and use that solution the next time the same objection comes up.

REFLECT

1. What do you think about a sales professional when you present them with an objection they cannot answer?

_____

_____

_____

_____

_____

2. Why do you believe you have procrastinated in the past when trying to uncover a solution to an objection that stumped you?

_____

_____

_____

_____

_____

_____

_____

3. What did you learn about yourself from this dare?

_____

_____

_____

_____

_____

_____

_____

4. If you consistently executed this process with every objection you encounter over the next year, how many sales would this dare earn you? Circle one:

1   2   3   4   5   6   7   8

WORK AS IF I'M NOT AFRAID OF OBJECTIONS

EFFORT

Rate your effort level towards improving yourself today with this dare:

1   2   3   4   5   6   7   8   9   10

_____

1: Did not read or do the dare. 2: Read the dare, but did not do it. 5. Did the dare with minimal effort. 10: Did the dare with 100% effort.

WEEK 6 SUMMARY

*B*efore you complete your journey, you need to take a moment to complete your Week 6 Summary. **You must do this in order to complete the "What's It Worth" equation on page 239.**

Average Effort Score for Week 6:

Review your Effort Scores from dares 26-40, and calculate your Average Effort Score for the week. Write it in the space below.

_____

What's it worth?

What was this week worth to you? Flip back through Week 6, and tally the number of sales that you said dares 36-40 would earn you. Write it below.

_____

You did it!

You completed all 40 dares!

Now turn the page to calculate the potential value of this program.

HOW MUCH EFFORT DID YOU GIVE?

Very quickly, go look up your Effort averages for Weeks 1-6, and write them in the spaces below.

_____**WEEK 1**

_____**WEEK 2**

_____**WEEK 3**

_____**WEEK 4**

_____**WEEK 5**

_____**WEEK 6**

Now, add up your scores and divide the total by 6 to calculate your average Effort Score for the whole program. Write your Effort Score below.

_____

Now you know how much you need to step up your effort in order to maximize the impact of *40 Day Sales Dare for Auto Sales* and achieve your full potential. If your average score is anything less than 10, then I strongly advise that you repeat the program for your benefit. Trust me on this. I want you to see how much you stand to gain if you were to keep applying the dares until you gave them 100% of your effort, so continue to the next page for some very important calculations.

WHAT'S IT WORTH?

What is this book worth to you? Flip back through your Summary Pages for Weeks 1-6, and calculate the total number of sales that you could earn if you executed all forty dares with 100% effort. Write your total below.

**If I follow everything in this book and give 100% effort,
I have the potential to earn _____ sales this year.**

**Now, calculate how much money you could earn if you executed
everything that you learned from *40 Day Sales Dare for Auto Sales*:**

_____ **× $**_____ **= $**_____

# of sales you have	your average	What you
the potential to	commission	could earn
earn by executing	per car	
all forty dares		

To fully realize the meaning of that potential, I want you to complete the sentence below and answer the question that follows:

**If I follow everything in this book and give 100% effort,
I have the potential to earn $ _____ .**

What would this money mean to you and your family?

_____

_____

_____

_____

WHAT IS THIS BOOK WORTH TO YOU?
I WANT TO KNOW!

Send me an e-mail and tell me how much money you have the potential to earn as a result of *40 Day Sales Dare for Auto Sales*. Feel free to share what these earnings would mean to you and your family, and what you plan to do in order to make this a reality. And, when you reach your goal, I want to hear about it!

If you want to reach this income goal, I believe you can do it if you commit to mastering the dares in this book and to giving 100% effort. If you'd like, you can simply go through the book again, and repeat the dares that you know you need to improve upon.

Or, you can make a fresh start and follow a new path through *40 Day Sales Dare for Auto Sales*. The topic outline on the next two pages divides the dares into four categories. By following this outline, you can concentrate on one major theme at a time. Also, this time around, you can set your own pace.

TOPIC OUTLINE

MENTAL MOTIVATION

UNDERSTANDING THE CUSTOMER'S MISSION TO IMPROVE THEIR LIFE

SOLVING THE CUSTOMER'S MISSION TO IMPROVE THEIR LIFE

HOLDING THE CUSTOMER ACCOUNTABLE TO ACHIEVING THEIR MISSION

ABOUT THE AUTHOR

JASON FORREST is a sales professional at heart, a speaker, and an expert at creating high-performance sales cultures through complete training programs. Jason incorporates experiential learning (rather than theory) to increase sales, implement cultural accountability, and transform companies into sales organizations. He is a member of the National Speaker's Association and was named one of 2012's Top Young Trainers for *Training* magazine—a national, industry-wide publication. Forrest is also the author of four previous books.

ABOUT FORREST PERFORMANCE GROUP

Forrest Performance Group (winner of Gold Stevie Award for Sales Training Program of the Year) specializes in culture change and creating urgency within sales teams and management. Forrest PG's competitive distinction is its behavior modification approach as applied to a variety of programs, education, seminars, and sales coach training offerings all aimed at dramatically improving sales force success.

Visit ForrestPG.com for more information.

Take your events and seminars
to the NEXT LEVEL with

JASON FORREST

TOPICS INCLUDE:

Transforming salespeople into
SALES PROFESSIONALS

Transforming managers into
COACHES

Transforming companies into
SALES ORGANIZATIONS

X FACTOR-BELIEFS

AND MORE!

LEADERSHIP SALES
COACHING

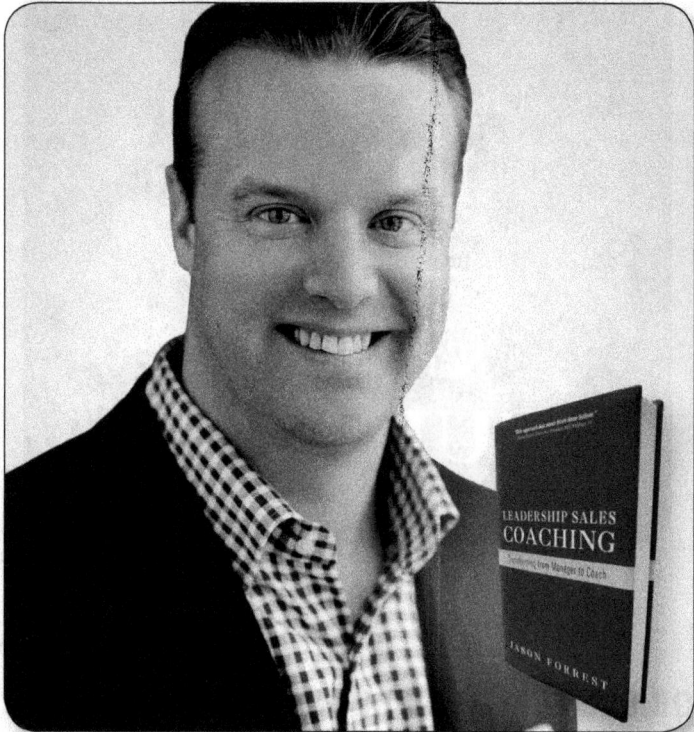

G et ready to learn the purpose of a sales coach with 75 principles that will transform you from a manager into a coach. In *Leadership Sales Coaching*, Jason shares the experience that comes with thousands of hours of seminars and coaching calls. Forrest's complete training program and coaching techniques have led his clients to transform from companies into sales organizations.

Driven by the core philosophy that when beliefs are in line, the right behaviors follow, this book is a must-have for any sales manager looking to lead his or her sales team to the next level and develop sales professionals into the best version of themselves.

ORDERING INFORMATION

To order *40 Day Sales Dare, Creating Urgency, Creating Urgency Unscripted, Leadership Sales Coaching,* and other income-increasing products, please visit us at:

www.ForrestPerformanceGroup.com/Store

For group sales (10 or more), contact Info@ForrestPG.com for bulk pricing.

TELL US YOUR STORY

Were you impacted by this book? After applying its principles, have you had any experiences that you would like to share?

At Forrest Performance Group, we're passionate about helping sales professionals transform the way they sell and the way they live. We'd love to hear from you!

Send your success stories, questions, and comments to Info@ForrestPG.com.

www.ForrestPG.com
817.886.0018

www.ingramcontent.com/pod-product-compliance
Lightning Source LLC
Chambersburg PA
CBHW060307100426
42742CB00011B/1889